Justice Transformation in Portugal

BUILDING ON SUCCESSES AND CHALLENGES

Please cite this publication as:
OECD (2020), *Justice Transformation in Portugal: Building on Successes and Challenges*, OECD Publishing, Paris, *https://doi.org/10.1787/184acf59-en*.

ISBN 978-92-64-46197-0 (print)
ISBN 978-92-64-49947-8 (pdf)

Photo credits: Cover © Ministry of Justice of Portugal.

Corrigenda to publications may be found on line at: *www.oecd.org/about/publishing/corrigenda.htm*.

Foreword

Justice sector performance is critical for achieving economic growth, citizen well-being and, more broadly, the Sustainable Development Goals. In recognition of its importance, Portugal has embarked on an ambitious agenda to guide the transformation of its justice sector.

As part of the OECD Initiative on Access to Justice for Inclusive Growth, this report takes stock of the Portuguese government's efforts to enhance the performance of the justice sector. It identifies results achieved so far, and it makes policy recommendations to support Portugal in providing justice services that meet the needs of citizens and businesses. In examining the Portuguese justice sector, the report draws on a set of OECD criteria for people-centred legal and justice service delivery, as well as on OECD work on regulatory and administrative simplification and digital government.

Building on several decades of reform, Portugal's current efforts – notably the *Justiça + Próxima* and *Simplex* + programmes – focus on making the justice sector more transparent, accessible and effective, by simplifying and dematerialising procedures and promoting innovation. As an example, the "Tribunal +" project and its pilot, the Court of Sintra, highlight how Portugal makes the most of digital technologies to transform courts. Portugal is one of the few countries adopting an integrated approach to making the justice sector more citizen-centred, through administrative simplification, improved services and digital strategies.

The report suggests ways to enhance further service integration, systems' interoperability and use of data, and procedural simplification and alignment. It formulates recommendations to promote the effectiveness and sustainability of the current reforms; these include strengthening co-operation and streamlining interactions across public agencies, for example through a shared vision of transformation and shared resources. Finally, the report highlights Portugal's strong potential for building on existing reforms to develop a comprehensive justice strategy across the different branches of power.

Acknowledgements

This report is published by the OECD Public Governance Directorate under the guidance of Marcos Bonturi, Director, and Irène Hors, Deputy Director. It was produced as part of the OECD work programme on Equal Access to Justice led by Tatyana Teplova, Head of Unit, Gender, Justice and Inclusiveness, and co-ordinated by Chloé Lelièvre, Justice Policy Analyst, OECD Public Governance Directorate.

The strategic guidance on the preparations of this report was provided by Irène Hors and Tatyana Teplova. Principal authors of this report are Francisco Cardona, international expert; Reza Lahidji, Partner, Menon Economics; Tatyana Teplova; Paula Fernando, Partner, Centre for Social Studies, University of Coimbra; Theresa Yurkewich and Chloé Lelièvre.

The OECD would like to thank the Government of Portugal, in particular the Ministry of Justice, for support in this project. Special thanks are due to Anabela Pedroso, State Secretary of Justice of Portugal for her leadership and dedicated work. Likewise, the authors are grateful for the views of Ministry of Justice experts, not least Pedro Tavares, Carolina Berto, Hugo Nunes, advisors to the State Secretary of Justice; Fátima Reis Silva, advisor to the Minister of Justice; and Miguel Romão, Director-General, Justice Policy, Portugal.

The content of the various chapters benefitted from research, comments and written input provided by Martyna Wanat, Policy Analyst, OECD Public Governance Directorate, and Luis Roman Arciniega Gil, Junior Researcher, University of Lille.

Logistical assistance was provided by Cicely Dupont-Nivore and editing by Eleonore Morena.

Table of contents

FIGURES

TABLES

BOXES

Follow OECD Publications on:

 http://twitter.com/OECD_Pubs

 http://www.facebook.com/OECDPublications

 http://www.linkedin.com/groups/OECD-Publications-4645871

 http://www.youtube.com/oecdilibrary

http://www.oecd.org/oecddirect/

Executive summary

Countries worldwide are seeking to transform their justice systems. Indeed, good governance, sound policy design and effective service delivery in justice institutions can contribute to a country's strong economic performance.

Like many OECD countries, Portugal is facing rising citizen expectations in terms of public sector performance, while experiencing low levels of public trust and confidence. These trends also affect the justice system, with people demanding greater efficiency and transparency, faster and more streamlined proceedings, and user-centred and responsive services. Meeting these demands requires new thinking and innovative practices that place the needs of people and businesses at the heart of justice institutions, policies and services.

In response to these pressures, Portugal has developed an ambitious agenda to guide the transformation towards a citizen-centred justice sector. Multiple reforms over the past two decades have sought to make the judiciary more transparent, accessible and effective. With its most recent reforms, "Justiça + Próxima" and "Simplex +", Portugal has adopted an integrated approach to administrative simplification, service improvement and digital strategies.

Under the *Justiça + Próxima* programme, Portugal aims to increase transparency and trust in justice institutions by simplifying and digitizing procedures, promoting justice innovation, and bringing the institutions closer to citizens. It has put in place over 170 constantly evolving and updated measures, which were designed through an innovative, collaborative and bottom-up process carried out with various justice stakeholders and citizens.

Portugal has also invested in the development of alternative dispute resolution mechanisms (i.e. arbitration, mediation and justices of the peace), which are becoming increasingly popular among citizens. The forthcoming common management platform for justices of the peace in consumer disputes, arbitration centres and public mediation systems (ADR +) will provide a strong basis for developing a holistic justice ecosystem, in line with the OECD criteria on people-centred justice services.

As part of the *Justiça + Próxima* programme, the *Tribunal +* project - including its pilot the Court of Sintra - promotes a greater use of technology in the courts as well as the rationalisation of internal and user processes. The project is generally appreciated by court staff, lawyers and court users, although citizens still need to come to court in person to obtain most information.

More broadly, Portugal continues its efforts to optimise the delivery of justice. For example, it has recently introduced a new model of court management to improve resource management and good governance. In addition, further to the multiple judicial map reforms carried out in recent years, a series of measures are planned to improve access to justice, including re-evaluating the judicial map, reopening several small courts and strengthening court infrastructure and capacities for video conferencing. Effective implementation of these measures will be critical to alleviate concerns about the growing concentration and centralisation of courts.

Overall, the current reforms of the justice system in Portugal, specifically the *Justiça + Próxima* programme (including the *Tribunal +* project), have a strong potential to transform the way in which the justice sector works. Recent data suggest that the Portuguese courts have made substantial efficiency gains, with the duration of court proceedings dropping from 417 days in 2010 to 289 days in 2016 on average. Trust in justice systems has also increased from 35% in 2014 to 44% in 2018 (CEPEJ data). Yet, as highlighted in the *2019 OECD Economic Survey of Portugal*, trials are still long compared to other OECD countries, with more than one-third of cases taking over a year to resolve. Moreover, trust in the system remains generally low. There is also a limited understanding of the extent to which current services can meet the needs of different groups of people and businesses.

In order to reap the full benefits and ensure the sustainability of the court modernisation reforms, it is important to further institutionalize them in policies, internal regulations, budgets and other dimensions of the justice system. There is also scope to enhance the involvement of the judiciary and individual judges in court transformation, process simplification and strengthening of human resources (i.e. legal clerks and assistant judges). Targeted judicial training could help improve the effectiveness of the 2013 judicial specialisation reforms. In addition, Portugal may also consider granting greater autonomy to court presidents, to improve efficiency in court management and support the achievement of the objectives for which they are accountable, and strengthening the powers of the Judicial Councils in the management of the judicial branch.

Providing stronger incentives for the use of alternative dispute resolution (ADR) processes (e.g. through greater court intervention), expanding them to other areas (e.g. commercial mediation), and improving the resolution of enforcement cases (including contract enforcement and insolvency proceedings) could further enhance the timeliness and efficiency of court processes.

Looking ahead, Portugal may consider developing a long-term and comprehensive justice strategy that brings together different branches of power and integrates different reform elements. Such a strategy should be based on a solid governance framework and could provide a platform for strengthening the overall justice infrastructure, and, ultimately, create a people-centred, seamless justice ecosystem. The strategy should be underpinned by a clear and evidence-based understanding of who needs justice the most, their legal problems and the impediments that they face in resolving these problems.

Summary analysis

MAIN FINDINGS	KEY RECOMMENDATIONS
Long term justice strategy	
Justice strategy – Need for a strategic reflection on the broader justice improvement needs, including with the involvement of the full range of stakeholders across the branches of power.	• Develop a longer-term inclusive and comprehensive justice strategy that brings together different branches of power respond to the legal needs of users across the country.
Legal needs – Need to deepen the understanding of diverse legal needs of citizens and business and how/whether the current services are able to fully respond to them.	• Strengthen the use of evidence-based and quantitative research methodologies as a basis for legal reform, including through better mapping and using legal needs surveys and public data.
User centred services – While improving, legal assistance, legal aid and various mechanisms for resolving disputes, including courts and ADR mechanisms, remain largely disconnected from each other and from other service delivery portals.	• Strengthen a user-centred and integrated approach as part of a continuum of dispute resolution services, in line with the *OECD criteria for people-centred legal and justice services* (including legal assistance, private bar, referrals, ADR and ODRs).
Use of technology – Building on the current reforms, there is a need for continued developing an integrated case management system for courts and different types of ADRs.	• Pursue the development of a common case management platform for ADR mechanisms and courts. • Consider evolving this platform into a single legal and dispute resolution service delivery window for business and people.
Data strategy for the justice sector – The granularity of court-level data remains limited and limited data collection efforts for private ADR mechanisms remain.	• Develop a holistic data strategy for the justice sector, encompassing the entire legal and justice chain, as well as maximise the use of data needed from other sectors. • Develop common data management protocols and strengthen its availability in different public and private systems for ADR.
Procedural simplification – Building on the current efforts, a need to continue streamlining complex laws and regulations, frequent changes in the legislation and non-legislative measures remains.	• Consider establishing inter-institutional working groups to review existing procedural laws and ensure their full alignment, including with ADR and people-centric approaches. They could also evaluate non-legislative measures (e.g. resource allocation and technological improvements).
Sustainability of reforms	
Monitoring and evaluation – Need for assessment of effects of measures in the Justiça + Próxima plan beyond organisational boundaries of the courts, such as user satisfaction, trust in justice institutions and citizens' broader access to justice.	• Design a robust analytical framework for the monitoring and evaluation of Justiça +Próxima and Tribunal+, which would be based on a detailed theory of change and enhanced data collection processes.
Tribunal + - Complexity of interactions among different agencies and differential capacities, resources and infrastructure in courts across the country, which can hamper the effectiveness of the roll out efforts if remain unaddressed.	• Enhance cooperation and streamline interactions across agencies in the justice chain, including judiciaries, prosecutors and others such as public and judicial ADR mechanisms. • Roll out Tribunal + project across the country, with the due attention to the court capacities and capabilities.
Judicial performance	
Judicial Capacity and performance - Judges in Portugal tend to be responsible for both the adjudication and auxiliary tasks, which is likely to contribute to procedural delays.	• Strengthen human resources in court support functions (e.g., paralegals, assistant judges) who can assist magistrates on substantive matters and by making the interface with the clerks.
Judicial processes and decision making – Limited autonomy of court presidents to make decisions on resource allocation.	• Review decision-making scope and resource allocation autonomy of court presidents to ensure sound court management and performance.
Judicial specialisation - While specialisation was in many instances achieved through specialised "local sections or branches", there is a need for greater specialised training and capacity building in specific areas of law for greater impact of specialisation efforts.	• Strengthen judicial specialisation, including through developing a comprehensive strategy in this area, updating the training needs of judges and staff, and enhancing focus on specialisation in commercial and economic matters, including international investment law.
Judicial map and court capacities – perception of growing concentration and centralisation of courts, in view of distance between courts and some population living in remote areas. Differentiated capacities of Courts across Portugal.	• Continue reviewing the judicial map taking into account access to justice by the most vulnerable citizens. • Continue efforts to strengthen managerial efficiency and the capacities of courts (e.g. infrastructure, IT, human and financial).

MAIN FINDINGS	KEY RECOMMENDATIONS
Enforcement and insolvency cases still account for much of the backlog in the Portuguese court system.	• Continue efforts to improve the resolution of insolvency and enforcement cases, including contract enforcement by controlling indicators such as trial length.
Alternative Dispute resolution	
Need to deepen the coherence, integration and responsiveness of different ADR mechanisms to users' needs.	• Develop an integrated strategy for ADR, through mediation, conciliation, justices of peace, ombudschemes, arbitration and other mechanisms. • Expand mediation to other areas, while strengthening the capacity of service providers and raising awareness among different stakeholders. • Strengthen the efficiency of peace courts through greater clarity of jurisdiction and meritocracy of decision-making.

Assessment and recommendations

Long-term justice strategy

The Justiça + Próxima programme (along with other programmes such as Simplex + and Capitalizar) aims to develop a justice that is swift, transparent, human and closer to the citizen, through simplification and dematerialisation of procedures, use of interoperable technologies, enhancing clarity, transparency and quality of information on laws and procedures and promoting justice innovation and modernisation. The current process for identifying modernisation measures represents an innovative and bottom-up effort, with input from a wide range of stakeholders. This process allowed to identify immediate gaps and develop measures to achieve quick successes in the improvement of the justice system from the perspective of users.

At the same time, some of these measures remain relatively ad hoc, with their implementation mainly linked to the electoral cycle and current government programme. There is also scope to deepen a reflection process on the broader judicial and justice reform needs (including internal human resources, financial and court management in the judiciary, balance of powers, co-ordination across justice actors, etc). In addition, there is currently an uneven understanding of the diversity of legal needs of citizens and business and the ability of the current justice services (e.g. courts, ADR mechanisms, legal assistance) to effectively respond to them.

Building on current efforts, a full transformation of the justice sector in Portugal will require a holistic and long-term approach to justice reforms. Such an approach should combine both institutional and policy transformation – across branches of power and the full chain of justice and legal institutions (courts, ADR mechanisms, the prosecution service, the legal profession, legal aid, enforcement agents, etc). It should also be based on the robust evidence related to legal needs, including those groups of individuals who may currently be left outside of the justice system and may not have access to courts or benefit from legal assistance.

Key recommendations

- Develop a longer-term inclusive and comprehensive justice strategy, which brings together different branches of power and goes beyond the electoral cycle to respond to the legal needs of people, businesses and other users across the country, including vulnerable groups.
- Strengthen the use of evidence-based and quantitative research methodologies as a basis for legal reform, including through better mapping of legal needs using legal needs surveys and administrative data.

User-centred services

Under the Justiça + Próxima programme, Portugal has also adopted a number of important initiatives to promote user-centricity of justice services, including through the increasing use of technology (e.g. establishing an online integrated case management system, promoting a range of alternative mechanisms to resolve disputes). The Portuguese authorities are also currently reviewing the legal aid framework with a view to enhancing its effectiveness. At the same time, legal assistance, legal aid and various mechanisms for resolving disputes (e.g. courts, mediation) appear to be disconnected from the understanding of the needs of users and have a limited connection to each other and to other service delivery portals for citizens and businesses.

Building on the current reforms, Portugal can maximise the impact of its current efforts to provide user-centred services by promoting further service integration and accessibility and by further mobilising technological capabilities, including through emerging technologies (such as artificial intelligence and blockchain) to build a seamless, people-centred legal and justice ecosystem. In line with good practices increasingly found in OECD countries, such an ecosystem could integrate both judicial and alternative mechanisms to resolve disputes, support effective triage of cases and enable multichannel dispute resolution avenues. This would call for common platforms for both case management and delivering of the full spectrum of legal and justice services.

In addition, there is scope for Portugal to link various legal advice and dispute resolution mechanisms to the existing citizens' service portal to facilitate early identification of problems and to provide a unique interface for citizens. Interoperability of data and big data could also help in this regard. The single digital Citizen Card and recently introduced Digital Mobile Key in Portugal could be extended to legal assistance and dispute resolution services to enable greater accessibility of such services and shift their focus on the preventive and restorative sides. Similarly, there is also scope to link dispute resolution mechanisms for businesses (e.g. commercial, investment, administrative, tax, labour) to the online portal of business-related services, in order to facilitate efficient resolution of disputes by businesses.

Key recommendations

- Strengthen a user-centred and integrated approach to the provision of legal assistance, legal aid, and dispute resolution services, including legal assistance, lawyers, referrals, ADR and online dispute resolution (ODR) as part of a continuum of dispute resolution services, in line with the OECD criteria for people-centred legal and justice services. This may include but is not limited to:
    - Developing an evidence-based service continuum by considering how different services fit together from the perspective of a user and by developing user-centred triage mechanisms, by taking into account a user pathway in moving from one dispute resolution mechanism to another and the required legal support at every stage of the process.
    - Establishing common platforms for court, ADR and legal aid/assistance services, which could provide a single portal for citizens and businesses and integrated case management systems for different types of dispute resolution mechanisms. This would serve as a strong basis for developing an integrated triage system for resolving disputes. This portal could be linked with both: i) the citizens' service portal, single digital Citizen's Card and Digital Mobile Key in Portugal; and ii) the business services portal.
    - Enhancing interoperability of information, through dematerialisation of data support and introduction of e-channels between courts, other justice institutions and other entities as the social security, health, education and security sectors.

- Assess the implementation and impact of the current setup of legal infrastructure (e.g. legal assistance, legal aid, court fees), along with the continuum of dispute resolution mechanisms to ensure – in an evidence-based manner – that it responds to the needs of those citizens and businesses.

Use of technology

Portugal recognises the need for strengthening the use of technology both for the improvement of case management, functioning of front and back offices in courts and service delivery to different clients. To this end, the Justiça + Próxima programme includes a range of measures to strengthen the current digital platforms for case management in ordinary (Citius +) and administrative/fiscal (SITAF) courts. In addition, the programme has introduced a Strategic Multi-Year 2018-28 Plan for improvement and modernisation of courts, which – among others – includes measures to strengthen the use of technology in courts. While currently there is no integrated case management system for courts and different types of ADRs, efforts are underway to create a common platform.

Looking ahead, technology must continue to be used as part of the daily functioning of the courts and the broader justice system if all the investment is to pay off. The ongoing efforts as part of the Justiça + Próxima programme provide a basis for establishing online systems that could support the resolution of disputes (i.e. provide actual services for obtaining legal advice and resolve disputes online). These systems could help diagnose legal problems of citizens and businesses, and inform them about their rights and options in order to help protect them and resolving their disputes.

In addition, continued efforts for the modernisation and simplification of procedures – across the entire justice sector, including ADRs and legal assistance/aid – will be essential in developing a justice ecosystem, which puts the needs of people at the centre. The forthcoming case management platform ADR + could provide an excellent basis for the development of such an ecosystem in Portugal. Portugal is also encouraged to continue its efforts to maximise the use of technology to promote accessibility of legal information, advice and resolution of disputes.

Key recommendations

- Continue improving design and functioning of justice information systems (e.g. enabling judges or public prosecutors to open a case and perform procedural acts in Citius without the prior intervention of a clerk; advancing the development of SITAF within the administrative and fiscal jurisdiction, combined with the process of rethinking and streamlining of procedures, also as part of Simplex +).
- Pursue the development of a common case management platform for ADR mechanisms and courts. Consider evolving this platform into a single legal and dispute resolution service delivery window for businesses and people.

Data strategy for the justice sector

While successive judicial reforms have increased the reliability and granularity of court-level data in Portugal, they have also introduced some discontinuities in the data that make the analysis of recent trends more challenging. Further changes are currently being introduced, although the granularity of court-level data remains limited. In addition, there are limited data collection efforts for private ADR mechanisms, in particular mediation, although there are ongoing efforts to improve the quality and availability of data in this area (including through ADR + platform).

Building on the current data collection efforts, there is scope to develop a holistic data strategy, which would include more granular longitudinal data (e.g. broken down according to the complexity of cases, the cost of litigation) to fully assess the impacts of different changes introduced as part of the recent reforms and have a better understanding of the efficiency of Portugal's courts.

To bridge separate public and private systems for arbitration and mediation and to strengthen the availability of data, it would be important to develop common data management protocols for the different ADR mechanisms.

Key recommendations

- Develop a holistic data strategy for the justice sector (encompassing the entire legal and justice chain, maximising the use of data needed from other sectors, including open data).
- Continue efforts to strengthen the granularity and usage of the available data across the justice sector.
- Develop common data management protocols and strengthen the availability of data in different public and private systems for arbitration and mediation.

Procedural simplification

While businesses greatly welcomed recent justice transformation efforts, they underlined the importance of addressing the complexity of laws, regulations and processes, as well as frequent changes in the legislation. Indeed, a series of successive procedural changes and reforms may require a holistic approach to reviewing the current stock of procedural legislation and regulations to remove any inconsistencies, complexities and overlaps.

Portugal may consider addressing the complexity of procedural legislation and judicial processes, capacity building of all justice stakeholders and undertaking a system-thinking approach to address the complex institutional and technological choices. Further alignment of procedural codes (civil, criminal and administrative) with a simpler, more efficient and people-centred justice as an objective could be beneficial, in view of their alterations as a result of various waves of reforms.

Key recommendations

- Consider establishing inter-institutional working groups to review existing procedural laws, to ensure their full alignment, including with the growing importance of ADR mechanisms and people-centric approaches. They could, in addition, evaluate non-legislative measures, such as resource allocation and technological improvements.

Monitoring and evaluation

Portugal is currently putting in place a common framework to monitor progress and evaluate the implementation of all measures included in Justiça + Próxima, including Tribunal +. Yet the assessment of effects of most measures in the Justiça + Próxima plan mainly focuses on direct savings of operational costs (e.g. savings on the cost of post stamps) and human resources.

For Tribunal +, the current indicators cover the main categories of benefits identified as a result of the implementation of the project. For the effective rollout of the project and for monitoring its performance, it would be important to explicitly integrate aspects that are beyond the organisational boundaries of the courts, such as user satisfaction, trust in justice institutions and citizens' broader access to justice.

In this regard, Portugal may consider elaborating a general analytical approach for ensuring that the evaluation and monitoring of both the programme Justiça +Próxima and Tribunal + are both consistent and comprehensive. This approach should be based on a detailed logical framework (or theory of change) that would spell out the causal linkages between its key measures and their direct and indirect outcomes and ultimate impact. Such a framework could be used to identify and assess external factors that could potentially influence outcomes, locate possible bottlenecks for efficiency gains, and orient methodological and data collection choices in future monitoring and evaluation activities. It could be accompanied by enhanced data collection and measurement of impacts, both on user practices and satisfaction.

Key recommendations

- Design a robust analytical framework for the monitoring and evaluation of Justiça +Próxima and Tribunal +, which would be based on a detailed theory of change and enhanced data collection processes.

Enhancing the sustainability of Tribunal + reforms

Overall, an important achievement of the Tribunal + project is to be appreciated by the judiciary staff, by lawyers and by court users. Yet, while the *judges* positively evaluated the reforms associated with Tribunal +, they stressed the importance of training, continued improvement of the new information system, and greater reflection on the current structure of human resources (such as the support staff to judges).

For the lawyers, while the assessment of reforms is positive both on behalf of their clients and on their own, they identified a number of process-related areas for improvement (e.g. need to accept different legal means of identification (including driver's licences, or residence permits for foreigners), which were no longer considered valid to access the courts), which could facilitate the accessibility and responsiveness of courts.

Businesses, in turn, welcomed the introduction of online services for dealing with some aspects of dispute resolution, although they emphasised the importance of greater communication of these reforms to enable better familiarity with the introduced changes.

More broadly, the Tribunal + project so far focused on sectors under the direct responsibility of the Ministry of Justice and have not directly addressed the work of judges, which may undermine the efficiency gains of the reforms. In addition, to support the scaling-up process, it would be important to increase the institutionalisation of the reform approach, strengthen the capacity of the resource team and enhance ownership by various institutional stakeholders in order to ensure sustainability and lasting impacts of reforms.

Fragmentation and complexity of interactions among different agencies were noted among the risks, which could affect the effectiveness of the ongoing reforms. Another key challenge is the need to adapt to different capacities, resources and infrastructure of courts across the country, which may slow down the rollout phase.

To address the remaining challenges and to maximise the impacts of the reforms, there is scope to enhance a user perspective in the design of the reforms through greater engagement of lawyers, businesses and regular citizens, in order to identify elements considered important from the user perspective. To fully reap the benefits of the Tribunal + project, there is also scope for greater involvement of judges in new ways of working and strengthening innovation and digital skills, which could also strengthen the levels of take-up by all staff.

Moreover, ensuring the sustainability of Tribunal + reforms requires attention to their institutionalisation in policies, internal regulations, budgets and other dimensions of the justice system. To this end, Portugal is encouraged to continue its current efforts to set up a management structure that would allow working across different institutions (e.g. the judiciary, Ministry of Justice [Administration of the Ministry of Justice, DGAJ], the Institute for Financial Management and Justice Equipment [IGFEJ], Office of the State Secretary, etc.) towards shared outcomes.

Another important measure to implement would be to strengthen co-operation and streamline interactions across agencies including judiciaries, prosecutors and others such as public and judicial ADR, through a shared vision of justice transformation, potentially accompanied by shared resources (e.g. human, material and financial resources), in order to help avoid unnecessary costs and inefficiencies.

Finally, in rolling out the components of Tribunal + throughout the country, it would be important to take proper account of the specific conditions and constraints of each local court, ensuring appropriate capacity of the resource team to support scaling up, integrating lessons learned for improvement from the implementation and evaluation of the Sintra project and enhancing communication of these reforms.

Key recommendations

- Strengthen the involvement of court users in the design and assessment of the ongoing rollout of the Tribunal + project. These efforts should be accompanied by greater communication of reforms to enhance understanding and familiarity of the introduced changes.
- Consider the extension of the project to cover the work of judges (in collaboration with the High Councils), including training, further adaptation of information systems, new methods of work with the clerical staff, and the development of a new category of support staff.
- Strengthen the institutionalisation of the reforms in policies, internal regulations, budgets and other dimensions of the justice system by engaging with appropriate institutions (i.e. DGAJ, IGFEJ).
- Enhance co-operation and streamline interactions across agencies in the justice chain, including judiciaries, prosecutors and others such as public and judicial ADR mechanisms.
- Roll out Tribunal + project across the country, with the due attention to be court capacities and capabilities.

Judicial capacity and performance

Judges in Portugal (except in the Supreme Court) tend to be responsible for both adjudication and auxiliary tasks (such as case preparation and management, research, and drafting of administrative documents), which is likely to generate procedural delays in the case management. In addition, performance appraisals of judges have been traditionally focused on qualitative criteria, although a number of quantitative indicators (e.g., productivity) were also in use (and were formalised in 2016 by the High Council of the Judiciary).

To this end, there is potential scope to speed up judicial decision-making if judges are supported by legal assistants/clerks. In this light, Portugal could benefit from continuous development of the judicial human resources model, e.g. by creating a new category of personnel to support judges in their substantive tasks.

In addition, Portugal may consider introducing transparent and negotiated case weighting criteria and more or less automated distribution of cases, within the limits of the principle of "natural judge". There is also room to continue reflecting on the balance between qualitative and quantitative performance indicators for judicial evaluation, in line with international good practices.

Key recommendations

- Strengthen human resources in court support functions (e.g. paralegals, assistant judges) which can assist magistrates on substantive matters (such as verifying the jurisprudence) and by liaising with the clerks.

- Consider strengthening transparent and negotiated case-weighting criteria, within the limits of the principle of "natural judge".
- Continue ongoing review of judicial performance evaluation criteria to ensure that they reflect the right balance between qualitative and quantitative criteria.

Judicial processes and decision-making

While Portugal has recently introduced a new model of court management, which aims to improve the efficiency of court management, the autonomy of court presidents to make decisions on resource allocation (e.g. human, financial, case flow management) within courts appears to be limited. In order to maximise court performance and in line with international practices, Portugal may consider reviewing levels of autonomy of court presidents, including financial autonomy and budget management.

Key recommendations

- Review decision-making scope and resource allocation autonomy of court presidents to ensure sound court management and performance.

Judicial specialisation

While specialisation in Portuguese judiciary was in many instances achieved through specialised "local sections or branches" (e.g. commercial, labour), in view of the increasing complexity of cases, judges could benefit from greater specialised training and capacity building in specific areas of law. In this context, Portugal could consider strengthening judicial specialisation, for example, in commercial and investment law, which could make the judicial system of Portugal more effective in these areas.

Key recommendations

- Develop a comprehensive strategy towards specialisation including updating the training needs of judges and staff.
- Strengthen specialisation, especially in commercial and economic matters, including international investment law.

Judicial map and court capacities

The structure of the judicial map has undergone multiple reforms over the last years in Portugal, including the 2013 reform, which consolidated the country's 231 judicial courts of first instance into 23 district clusters. The Justiça + Próxima programme envisages a series of measures to further optimise the judicial map, which aim to alleviate some concerns about the growing concentration and centralisation of courts, in view of shortening the distance between the courts and parts of the population living in remote areas.

In addition, courts across Portugal are reported to have varying capacities to deal with the workload and provide access to justice (e.g. infrastructure, information technology [IT], human and financial). To this end, a Strategic Multi-Year 2018-28 Plan for Improvement and Modernisation of Courts includes measures to strengthen various court capacities to be rolled out over a ten-year period.

Looking ahead and to build on current efforts, authorities are encouraged to continue re-evaluating the judicial map and strengthening court capacities for video conferencing and other equipment and identifying ways to improve human and financial resources.

Key recommendations

- Continue reviewing the judicial map, taking into account both access to justice by the most vulnerable citizens, including those dwelling in rural areas, and managerial efficiency.
- Continue efforts to strengthen court capacities (financial, human, infrastructure, IT, etc).

Enforcement cases

The number of completed enforcement cases has consistently exceeded cases entering the system (whose number has been declining since the crisis years) along with the processing times. Yet, enforcement cases still account for much of the backlog in the Portuguese court system.

In this regard, it would be important for Portugal to continue its efforts to improve the resolution of enforcement cases, as they are essential for businesses.

Key recommendations

- Continue efforts to improve the resolution of enforcement and insolvency cases, including contract enforcement by controlling indicators such as the length of the proceedings.

Alternative dispute resolution mechanisms

In Portugal, alternative dispute resolution (ADR) mechanisms, i.e. arbitration, mediation and justices of peace, are becoming increasingly popular and are part and parcel of the latest modernisation efforts. Yet there is scope to deepen the coherence, integration and responsiveness of different ADR mechanisms to client needs, which could help parties bring their dispute to the right forum.

In addition, while the public mediation system is becoming widely popular in Portugal, service satisfaction remains the lowest among all ADRs. The capacities and take-up across a wide range of areas also remain low. Finally, while the availability of justices of the peace is increasing in Portugal, they remain limited in use. Stakeholders also raised concerns regarding the meritocracy of their decisions and potential jurisdictional overlap. Developing a people-centred justice service ecosystem requires countries to find ways to integrate ADR along with other resolution processes in a coherent and holistic justice sector vision while maintaining their empowerment. There is strong potential to facilitate the development of such an ecosystem in Portugal with ADR +, the forthcoming case management platform. This initiative will aim to provide a common stage for justices of the peace in consumer dispute arbitration centres and public mediation systems. There is also scope to integrate other mechanisms, such as Ombud schemes and conciliation.

Portugal may also benefit from enhancing the level of resources and facilities in order to increase the speed of mediation. Further efforts to increase the take-up of mediation – possibly through strengthening incentives and communication (e.g. through greater court intervention) and expand to other areas (e.g. commercial mediation) would be beneficial in order to reach its full potential. Collecting data from private mediation systems would also allow mapping the extent of the popularity of this mechanism.

Finally, there is scope to strengthen the mechanism of justices of the peace by ensuring that there is no overlap with other jurisdictions, greater efficiency and merit-based decision-making.

Key recommendations

- Develop an integrated strategy for alternative dispute resolution (ADR), through mediation, conciliation, justices of the peace, Ombud schemes, arbitration and other mechanisms.

- Expand mediation to other areas (e.g. commercial mediation), while strengthening the capacity of service providers and raising awareness among different stakeholders.
- Strengthen the efficiency of peace courts through greater clarity of jurisdiction and meritocracy of decision-making.

1 Modernising justice for inclusive growth: Leaving no one behind

This chapter provides an overview of a justice reform agenda in Portugal with a particular focus on measures aimed at modernisation, innovation capacity and strengthening citizen-centric approaches to access to justice.

Putting people at the centre of an innovative justice system

The transformation of justice institutions is a pressing necessity for many countries around the world. Their governance, policy design and service delivery can contribute to the efficiency of a country's justice system. Citizens and businesses expect better and faster results, and more responsive, targeted and effective services, including access to legal information, legal assistance and dispute resolution. This requires new thinking, innovative ways of working, prioritising the needs of people at the centre of institutions, policy and service delivery frameworks – in the justice sector as well as in other policy areas.

In recent years, Portugal has seen the emergence of an increasingly ambitious agenda that has guided the transformation of the justice sector. The country is taking active steps towards modernising its justice system to ensure its inclusiveness and responsiveness to the needs of people. Multiple reforms in the past two decades have sought to make the justice sector more transparent, accessible and effective (Gomes, 2007; Dias and Gomes, 2018). The most recent initiatives include the Justiça + Próxima programme, which encompasses the Tribunal + flagship project, Court + as well as Simplex +, a cross-governmental modernisation plan. These initiatives are linked to the government's overall vision, which provides a solid anchoring in the development of the priorities in the country.

Through a combination of these efforts, Portugal has become one of the few countries actively introducing a comprehensive package of administrative simplification, digitalisation and innovation measures across the justice sector. With these reforms, Portugal demonstrates its commitment to the dissemination of a culture of innovation and people-centricity across the justice sector.

Yet, some of the challenges faced by justice systems, similar to other public service areas, include slow adoption of technology, often outdated and complex processes, and declining trust and confidence of people and businesses. This is particularly challenging as they involve independent judiciaries, prosecutors and other agencies, public, judicial and private alternative dispute resolutions (ADRs), including at different levels of government, and other stakeholders.

In addition, citizen expectations continue to rise as innovations in other sectors improve service delivery, while governments, courts, legal and other services, often struggle to keep up. For example, legal and justice services, not unlike other services, often rely on paper forms while many others are increasingly delivered in a mobile environment. Indeed, emerging evidence from a wide range of sectors suggests that one of the most effective ways to improve trust in government is by improving the quality of the government service delivered. Portugal recognises that it has a unique opportunity to transform its legal and justice services to become more people-centric and user-driven – with technology as a core enabler of service provision.

To this end, Portugal has approached the OECD to support the implementation of new measures aimed at modernisation and development of approaches that put people at the centre and create innovation capacity in Portugal's justice system, designing citizen-centric approaches to access to justice. This review *Justice Transformation in Portugal: Building on Successes and Challenges* seeks to take stock of the government transformation efforts, identify results and make policy recommendations aimed at enhancing the responsiveness and accessibility of legal and justice services with regards to the needs of citizens and economic actors. The analysis draws on policy documents, direct insights and information collected during a fact-finding mission and stakeholder interviews in the jurisdictions of Lisbon and Sintra in October 2018, as well as desk research. A preliminary draft was fact-checked and preliminary analysis was discussed and validated with governmental stakeholders in March 2019.

The review takes into account a set of OECD criteria for people-centred legal and justice service delivery, setting out guiding principles to support governments in designing and delivering more people-centred legal and justice services (Box 1.1).

It also builds on OECD work for regulatory and administrative simplification, digital government, effective governance and service delivery.

Box 1.1. OECD Criteria for people-centred legal and justice services

Evidence-based planning

People-centred legal and justice services are based on and respond to an empirical understanding of the legal needs and legal capabilities of those who require or seek assistance.

Accessibility

People-centred legal and justice services are accessible and designed to overcome actively the range of barriers to the assistance they require.

Availability

People-centred legal and justice services are available across the justice chain and provided in a range of formats, programme and service types.

Prevention, proactivity and timeliness

People-centred legal and justice services are proactive and contribute to the prevention of legal problems and a timely resolution. Recurring legal problems are addressed on a systemic basis to address underlying causes, thereby preventing reoccurrences.

Appropriateness and responsiveness

People-centred legal and justice services are appropriate and responsive to the individual, the issues they face and their situation. They are tailored, proportionate, efficient and flexible to accommodate local circumstances.

Empowerment

People-centred legal and justice services are empowering, enable people's meaningful participation in the justice system and build people's legal capabilities.

Equality and inclusion

People-centred legal and justice services are inclusive and targeted at those most in need, responsive to specific access needs of particular groups likely to suffer from social and economic disadvantage, of those who are otherwise marginalised or vulnerable and those with complex needs. They are designed to contribute to equality, poverty reduction and social inclusion.

Outcome focus and fairness

People-focused legal and justice services contribute to fair process and fair outcomes and to better and more sustainable procedural, substantive and systemic outcomes, including increased trust and confidence in the justice system and better justice system performance, and to the attainment of social objectives such as socioeconomic inclusion.

Collaboration and integration

People-centred legal and justice services are part of a coherent system that provides seamless referrals and integrated services through collaboration among legal, justice and other human service providers. People get access to all the services they need to solve the legal and related non-legal aspects of their problems holistically, regardless of the entry point for assistance.

Effectiveness

People-focused legal and justice services are effective and continually improved through evaluation, evidence-based learning and the development and sharing of best practices.

Source: OECD, (2019), Equal Access to Justice for Inclusive Growth: Putting People at the Centre, Paris, https://doi.org/10.1787/597f5b7f-en.

Justice transformation for people, communities and business

Towards people-centred justice ecosystems for the 21st century

Similar to most OECD countries, public institutions in Portugal have been facing rising citizen expectations of public sector performance and declining public trust and confidence. These trends affect the full chain of the justice sector, including courts, prosecutors, alternative dispute resolution (ADR) mechanisms and legal services – with people demanding greater efficiency and transparency of institutions, faster and more streamlined proceedings, more people-centred and more responsive services and better enforcement. As other OECD countries, Portugal inherited systems which are slow to change, based on complex practices, processes and procedures and outdated legacy information technology (IT) systems, which in many cases contributed to inefficient services, unnecessary duplication and increased margins of error, and hence suboptimal use of taxpayers' resources and low client satisfaction (such as victims and witnesses).

Furthermore, the growing complexity of criminal justice cases (e.g. white-collar and financial crimes, cyberattacks, online fraud and cybercrime) demands greater co-ordination, efficiency and data interoperability among different justice stakeholders. Such complexity also increases trial time, which can result in substantially greater numbers of backlogged cases.

In this context, Portugal, similar to many OECD countries, is taking active steps to make its justice system more accessible, efficient and responsive to the needs of people and businesses, also with a view to strengthening their transparency and trustworthiness. These efforts are also taking place in the context of tight financial constraints (Box 1.2), thus putting pressures on the government and the judiciary to identify new and innovative ways to deliver more and better services for less.

Box 1.2. Justice modernisation under the 2011 Memorandum of Understanding with the International Monetary Fund (IMF) and the European Union (EU)

With a view to stabilising public debt, Portugal signed, on 17 May 2011, a Memorandum of Understanding (MoU) on Specific Economic Policy Conditionality with the European Commission, the European Central Bank (ECB) and the IMF, known as the Troika. It required Portugal to implement a wide range of austerity measures over a three-year period, which extended to almost every area of governance, from social security to education, healthcare and justice. The MoU foresaw a number of measures (objectives) for the justice sector (Chapter 7), which aimed to:

1. Improve the judicial system by ensuring effective and timely enforcement of contracts and competition rules.
2. Increase efficiency by restructuring the court system and adopting new court management models.
3. Speed up judicial proceedings by reducing court backlogs and facilitating out-of-court dispute settlements.

In particular, the judicial system had to identify areas for cost-cutting and carry reforms with reduced resources (Dias, 2016, p. 34).

As a result of a wide range of reforms, the Troika approved Portugal's exit from the EUR 78 billion bailout and the IMF applauded the country for reforming the judicial system. Trends identified by the EU in 2017[1] marked that the reforms in the corporate insolvency and restructuring frameworks helped foster a stronger focus on companies' recovery by introducing out-of-court insolvency frameworks. The latest 2019 European Semester pointed out that the efficiency and performance of the Portuguese justice system significantly improves but still face challenges mainly in administrative, tax and insolvency proceedings, including the low-resolution rate, long duration of proceedings, uneven enforcement of rulings.

The austerity measures were seen as being associated with a number of challenges during that period, such as the shutdown of the court and case management system (Citius) for approximately two months in 2014 and the deteriorating physical condition of the buildings (Dias and Gomes, 2018).

Source: EC (2011), *Portugal - Memorandum of Understanding on Specific Economic Policy Conditionality*, http://ec.europa.eu/economy_finance/eu_borrower/mou/2011-05-18-mou-portugal_en.pdf; Dias, J.P. (2016), "The transition to a democratic Portuguese judicial system: (Delaying) changes in the legal culture", https://doi.org/10.1017/S1744552315000373; Dias, J.P. and C. Gomes (2018), "Judicial reforms "under pressure": The new map/organisation of the Portuguese judicial system", *Utrecht Law Review*, Vol. 14(1), pp. 174-86; EC (2017), "Country report Portugal 2017, including an in-depth review on the prevention and correction of macroeconomic imbalances", Commission staff working document, European Commission, https://ec.europa.eu/info/sites/info/files/2017-european-semester-country-report-portugal-en.pdf.; EC (2019), "Country Report Portugal 2019, including an in-depth review on the prevention and correction of macroeconomic imbalances", Commission staff working document, European Commission, https://ec.europa.eu/info/sites/info/files/file_import/2019-european-semester-country-report-portugal_en_0.pdf.

These justice improvement efforts are on the whole aligned with the broader trends in public modernisation across OECD countries, which involve the following shifts:

1. *More people-centred approaches in governance, policymaking and service delivery* – By reorienting policymaking, governance and service design processes towards people, their needs and preferences rather than institutions. This also involves efforts in co-creating and co-producing services and policies (which in turn calls for greater access to public data, availability of analytical tools, and mechanisms to monitor outcomes), which turn people into partners and collaborators. This requires balancing between internal improvements through greater efficiency and effectiveness of processes and meeting of external demand and needs.
2. *More simplified processes* – Effective design and delivery of services for the people calls for efforts to rethink and streamline the processes and procedures to facilitate user experiences in accessing legal and justice services. This requires getting under the skin of how courts, ADR mechanisms, legal aid and assistance processes operate and putting the needs of users at the centre.
3. *Greater innovation and digitalisation in service delivery* – Modernisation through simplification, innovation and technology hold great potential for improving public services and the public sector at large, including with regard to legal assistance and justice. This requires targeted efforts to

encourage an organisational culture which promotes innovation and development of an environment, allowing for the systematic generation of ideas.

In Portugal, justice sector modernisation efforts are taking place as part of broader efforts to strengthen quality and satisfaction with service delivery. For example, in 2018, in the area of digital public services, Portugal has demonstrated above-average performance in comparison to EU member states (EC, 2018b)[2] (Figure 1.1).

Moreover, with regard to online service completion (which refers to the share of administrative steps related to major life events that can be done online), Portugal has been among the top performers, which provides a solid foundation for expanding this approach to the justice sector (Figure 1.2).

A combination of these efforts to simplify and streamline the processes, innovation and technology, in turn, can improve and integrate services, reduce waiting times, enhance engagement of various stakeholders and improve management of cases by reducing the number of ineffective trials.

Trustworthy, effective and efficient justice institutions can guarantee fair proceedings and give legal certainty to citizens, businesses and investments. Indeed, the OECD Policy Framework for Investment (PFI) has pointed out that when conditions for access to justice are not guaranteed or are inefficient, such as the case of complex, costly and extensive judicial processes, the business sector, including small- and medium-sized enterprises (SMEs), may limit their commercial activities (OECD, 2015c). As such, the rule of law and timely legal and justice services offer opportunities for business to flourish, taking into account elements such as the level of impact on legal frameworks, research and development (R&D), access to financing, supplementary fair markets that channel resources to productive sectors, and any restructuring and displacement that may accompany them (OECD, 2018). The other way around, crime and violence combined with delayed and corrupt justice may have a negative impact on corporate projects and investment risks, thus affecting competitiveness and economic growth (OECD, 2018).

Figure 1.1. Digital Economy and Society Index (DESI) 2018, Digital public services in EU countries

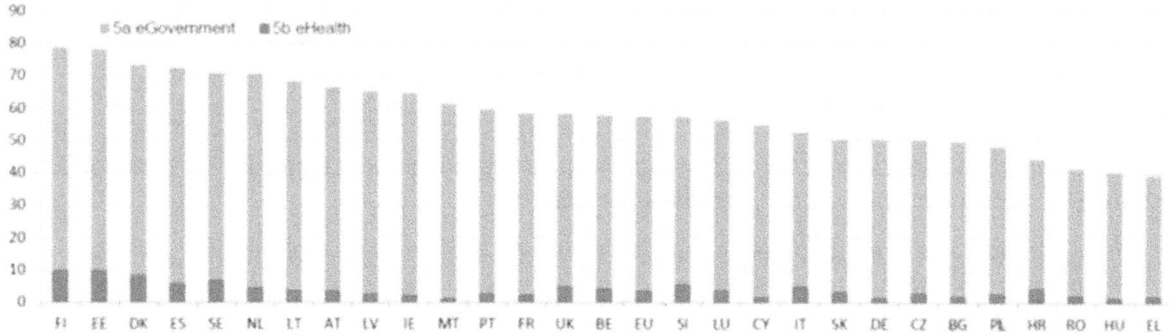

Source: EC (2018a), *DESI Report 2018 - Digital Public Services*, http://ec.europa.eu/newsroom/dae/document.cfm?doc_id=52244.

Figure 1.2. Online service completion in EU countries, 2016-17

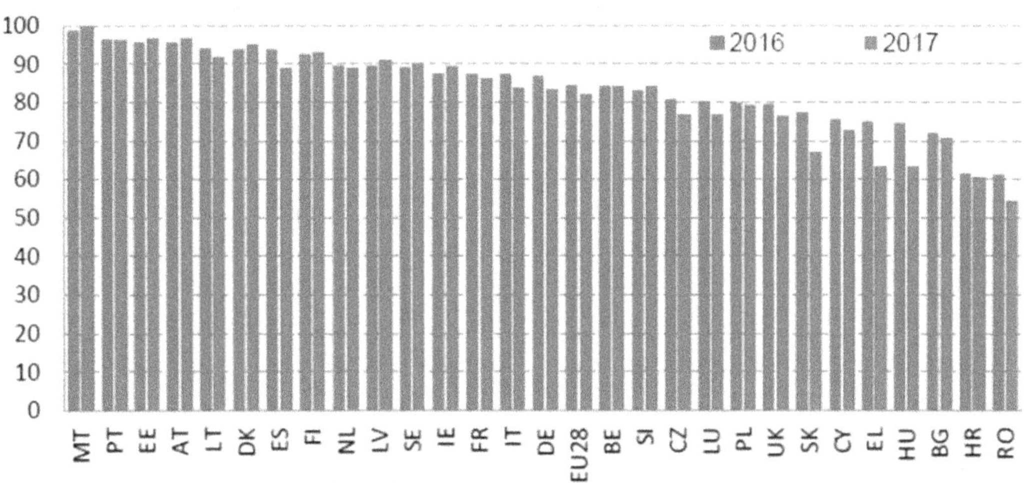

Source: EC (2018a), *DESI Report 2018 - Digital Public Services*, http://ec.europa.eu/newsroom/dae/document.cfm?doc_id=52244.

In addition, the modernisation of the justice sector provides a strong foundation to strengthen the responsiveness of justice and legal institutions services in meeting the legal needs of people and businesses (Box 1.3). A study carried out in 2015 by *Direção-Geral da Política de Justiça* (DGPJ) and the High Institute for Political and Social Sciences of the University of Lisbon highlighted that while the current legal aid and assistance system[3] ensures efficiency in guaranteeing access to justice, there could be scope for further improvement (e.g. assessing the relevance of the legal need, use of legal aid for ADRs, etc). As such, the Portuguese authorities are currently reviewing the legal aid framework, including through the review of the legislation. Having a thorough understanding of people's needs and experiences could support the authorities in these efforts to develop a modern legal need and assistance system (see Chapter 5).

Box 1.3. Legal needs in Portugal

In accordance with the global legal needs research, most people experience some forms of civil legal problems over the course of their life. As in other OECD countries, two-thirds of Portuguese respondents report experiencing at least one legal problem over the course of two years[4] (Figure 1.3). The most frequently mentioned problems relate to consumer issues, housing, money and public services. As in most countries, justiciable problems tend to particularly affect certain disadvantaged groups (e.g. recipients of social benefits, people from low-income groups). In all countries, legal problems expose people to direct and indirect impacts (e.g. a loss of employment or income opportunities, exposure to violence).

Source: Based on the information provided by the Government of Portugal and adapted by the OECD.

Figure 1.3. Share of respondents who report at least one justiciable problem

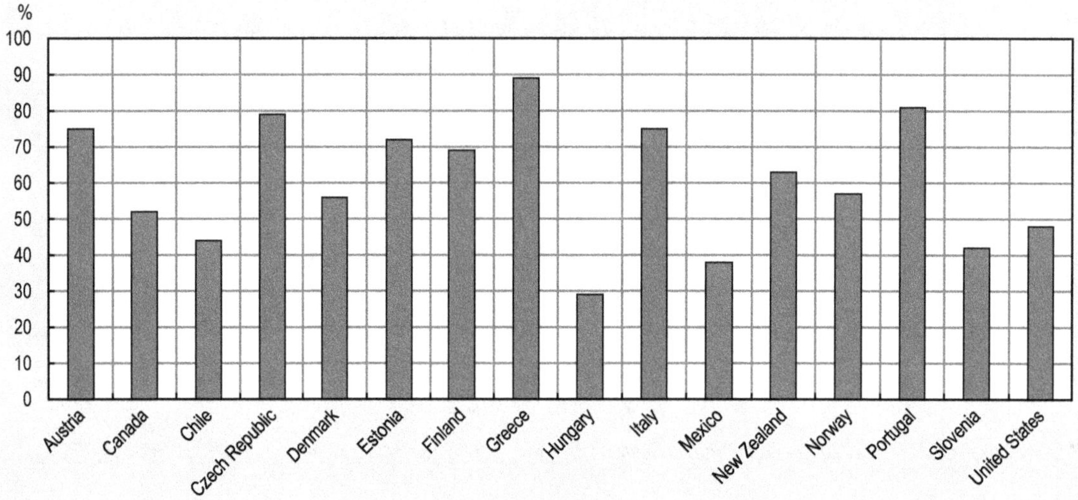

Note: Legal problem with a level of seriousness of 4 or more on a 0-10 scale.
Source: World Justice Project (2018), *Global Insights on Access to Justice: Findings from the World Justice Project General Population Poll in 45 Countries*, World Justice Project, Washington, DC; author's calculations.

There are also indications, that the share of legal needs that are met is higher in Portugal than in many comparable countries. At 30%, the share of respondents who lack legal capability (in the sense of not knowing where to obtain information and assistance to solve their legal problem) is lower than in most OECD countries. Importantly, one-fourth of respondents who faced a legal problem had received professional assistance, which constitutes one of the highest shares among OECD countries. However, access to professional advice seems to increase rather strongly with the level of income. Finally, 65% of the legal problems reported in the survey had been resolved, of which only 5% had been addressed through the formal legal system.

Source: World Justice Project (2018), *Global Insights on Access to Justice: Findings from the World Justice Project General Population Poll in 45 Countries*, World Justice Project, Washington, DC; OECD (2019), "Building a business case for access to justice", OECD White Paper.

Notes

[1] Under the economic adjustment programme for Portugal 2011-2014.

[2] The digital public services dimension consists of six indicators: the eGovernment users measured as a percentage of those Internet users who need to submit forms to the public administration (eGovernment users indicator); the extent to which data that is already known to the public administration is pre-filled in forms presented to the user (pre-filled forms indicator); the extent to which the various steps in dealing with the public administration can be performed completely online (online service completion indicator); the degree to which public services for businesses are interoperable and cross-border (digital public services for businesses indicator); the government's commitment to open data (open data indicator); and the percentage of people who used health and care services provided online without having to go to a hospital or doctors surgery (eHealth services indicator).

[3] Legal aid in Portugal is regulated by Law 34/2004 of 29 July (amended by Law 47/2007 of 28 August, Law 40/2018 of 08 August, and Decree-law 120/2018 of 27 December) and Ordinance 10/2008 of 3 January (amended by Ordinance 210/2008 of 29 February, 654/2010 of 11 August and 319/2011 of 30 December). Under such regulation, legal aid encompasses legal information (as a duty of the state to carry out activities to disseminate knowledge on the rule of law and on the legal regime) and legal protection. Legal protection comprises two strands: legal advice and legal assistance to a specific case brought before a court, a justice of the peace or an ADR centre as defined by a ministerial ordinance. Legal assistance, on the other hand, can be granted in the following types: i) exemption from court fees and other costs of the proceedings; ii) appointment of a lawyer and payment of his/her fees (according to a pre-established scheduled of fees approved by ministerial ordinance); iii) benefit of paying court fees and other costs of the proceedings by instalment; iv) appointment of a lawyer and benefit of paying fees by instalment, according to the same schedule of fees mentioned previously; and v) appointment of an enforcement agent.

Both legal advice and legal assistance are provided by lawyers enrolled, on a voluntary basis, in the legal aid system according to their preferential fields of practice. Legal advice or legal assistance is granted to persons or legal entities who meet the legal criteria for economic insufficiency and the types of legal assistance are granted according to the level of economic insufficiency.

The procedure among the different institutions that concur to provide legal aid relies on tailor-made information systems. The attribution of the benefit of legal advice or legal assistance is decided by the Social Security Institute and is supported by AJUDIC – an information system developed by the Social Security. Lawyers are appointed by the Bar Association, through an information system called SINOA (*Sistema de Informação da Ordem dos Advogados*) that allows lawyers to register the state of the case, to interact when necessary with the Bar Association (to ask to be excused from a case for example) and to request their fees at the end of the case. Lawyers' fees are paid by the state (according to a pre-established scheduled of fees approved by ministerial ordinance that takes into account the various types of cases) through the IGFEJ supported by another information system – the SICAJ (*Sistema de Confirmação dos Pedidos de Pagamento de Apoio Judiciário*).

[4] The key advantage of the General Population Poll (GPP) is to deploy the same methodology in all countries (World Justice Project, 2018). GPP results should be interpreted with caution due to the inherent limitations of surveys and the differences of institutional and cultural context between countries. As everyday issues might not represent a substantial legal need, the analysis is restricted to problems above a certain threshold of (reported) seriousness (in the sequel, justiciable problems are defined as problems with a reported level of seriousness of 4 or more in a scale going from 0 to 10).

References

Dias, J.P. (2016), "The transition to a democratic Portuguese judicial system: (Delaying) changes in the legal culture", in *International Journal of Law in Context*, Vol. 12(1), pp. 24-41, https://doi.org/10.1017/S1744552315000373.

Dias, J.P. and C. Gomes (2018), "Judicial reforms "under pressure": The new map/organisation of the Portuguese judicial system", *Utrecht Law Review*, Vol. 14(1), pp. 174-86.

EC (2019), "Country Report Portugal 2019, including an in-depth review on the prevention and correction of macroeconomic imbalances", Commission staff working document, European Commission, https://ec.europa.eu/info/sites/info/files/file_import/2019-european-semester-country-report-portugal_en_0.pdf.

EC (2018a), *DESI Report 2018 - Digital Public Services*, European Commission, http://ec.europa.eu/newsroom/dae/document.cfm?doc_id=52244.

EC (2018b), *The Digital Economy and Society Index (DESI)*, European Commission, https://ec.europa.eu/digital-single-market/en/desi.

EC (2017), "Country report Portugal 2017, including an in-depth review on the prevention and correction of macroeconomic imbalances", Commission staff working document, European Commission, https://ec.europa.eu/info/sites/info/files/2017-european-semester-country-report-portugal-en.pdf.

EC (2011), *Portugal - Memorandum of Understanding on Specific Economic Policy Conditionality*, European Commission, http://ec.europa.eu/economy_finance/eu_borrower/mou/2011-05-18-mou-portugal_en.pdf.

Gomes, C. (2007), "The transformation of the Portuguese judicial organization: Between efficiency and democracy", *Utrecht Law Review*, Vol. 3(1), pp. 101-11.

Ministry of Justice of Portugal (2015), *Early Impact Assessment Study on the Access to Law and the Courts*, Directorate-General for Justice Policy, https://dgpj.justica.gov.pt/Portals/31/Estudos%20AIN%20DGPJ/Estudo_acesso_ao_direito_maio_2015.pdf.

OECD (2019), "Building a business case for access to justice", OECD White Paper.

OECD (2018), Access to Justice for Business and Inclusive Growth in Latvia, OECD Publishing, Paris, https://doi.org/10.1787/9789264303416-en.

OECD (2015), *Policy Framework for Investment, 2015 Edition*, OECD Publishing, Paris, http://dx.doi.org/10.1787/9789264208667-en.

World Justice Project (2018), *Global Insights on Access to Justice: Findings from the World Justice Project General Population Poll in 45 Countries*, World Justice Project, Washington, DC.

2 Towards a smart justice system in Portugal

This chapter describes the main strategies and initiatives to drive justice transformation in Portugal. It focuses on promoting simpler, digital, open and innovative approaches and optimising justice service delivery.

Whole-of-public-sector approach to justice transformation

Vision for justice transformation in Portugal

In Portugal, recent years have seen the emergence of an ambitious programme to drive the transformation of the justice sector. Recent initiatives include the Justiça + Próxima programme and more specifically the Tribunal + project and the horizontal project, Simplex +.

Important examples prior to these efforts include: the 2008 Law on the Organisation and Functioning of Judicial Courts;[1] the measures taken within the context of the 2011 Memorandum of Understanding on financial assistance with the International Monetary Fund (IMF) and the European Union (EU), such as the new Code of Civil Procedure;[2] and the 2013 Law on the Organisation of the Judicial System[3] (Box 2.1).

Box 2.1. Civil Procedure Reform in Portugal

Reforms to civil procedure over the last 40 years can be divided into three different phases: i) from 1976 to 1994, with a democratisation period focusing on the adequacy of the civil procedure regime with regards to the new constitution and looked to speed up the procedure; ii) from 1995 to 2006, with a focus on procedural promptness; iii) from 2006 onwards, the procedural management period. During this last period, reforms have focused on procedural flexibility and management, aiming at a faster and more efficient justice.

The new Civil Procedure Code that entered into force in September 2013 through Law no. 41/2013 of 26 June,[4] aligns with these objectives. The main changes for the majority of the proceedings were the following: i) limitation of the number of pleadings in a proceeding; ii) simplification of the proceedings; iii) the possibility given to the judge to adapt the proceedings to the case.

As for the enforcement proceedings, the key changes introduced by the new code were to:

- Streamline the system of debt recovery, especially by direct electronic seizure of bank accounts of the debtor by the bailiffs (Articles 749 and 780).
- Speed up the enforcement of civil court rulings (Article 85).
- Terminate proceedings where debts were not recoverable, a measure that significantly reduced the backlog in courts (new Article 849) during the Troika period.[5]
- Allow cases to be closed in court without waiting for all pending payments to be made when only periodic payments are seized and the future incomes are adjudicated to the creditor (Article 779, 4, b). The case can be reopened if the creditor is not fully paid.
- Encourage the use of electronic auctions to sell seized assets (Article 837).

These changes are estimated to have allowed the closing and transfer of close to 250 000 cases between 2012 and 2014, out of a total of 1.7 million pending cases in 2012. According to the Portuguese authorities, the figure comes closer to 650 000 during the period 2012-16/17.

Source: Gouveia, M.F., J. Pinto-Ferreira and M. Teixeira (2017), "Evolução do processo civil: Democratização, celeridade e gestão processual", in M. de L. Rodrigues et al. (eds.), *40 Anos de Políticas de Justiça em Portugal*, Almedina, Coimbra, pp. 181-97.

The programmes seek to ensure that justice services are efficient, agile and innovative, but also accessible and humane. They also aim to upgrade the capacity of justice stakeholders, including courts, to interact with and respond to the needs of its constituents.

This and subsequent chapters take stock of the progress made by the Portuguese government on this journey, based on good practices in OECD countries. In particular, this chapter provides an overview of high-level strategies and approaches adopted by the Government of Portugal to modernise the justice sector, in line with the overall vision for an efficient, agile and user-centred public sector.

Strategy for justice transformation in Portugal

Portugal has been employing a sophisticated approach to the overall public sector transformation, including in the justice area (Figure 2.1). It is one of the OECD countries integrating elements of administrative simplification, service improvement and digital strategies, with a view to improving citizen-centricity in the justice sector. By following this approach in the justice area, Portugal is aspiring to transform the way that justice is delivered to people and businesses in order to:

- create a better business climate
- strengthen trust in justice institutions and improving the perception of justice
- strengthen the transparency of justice through improved service
- improve responsiveness and efficiency of services and meeting budget constraints
- bring justice closer to people.

Figure 2.1. Portugal's strategies for justice transformation

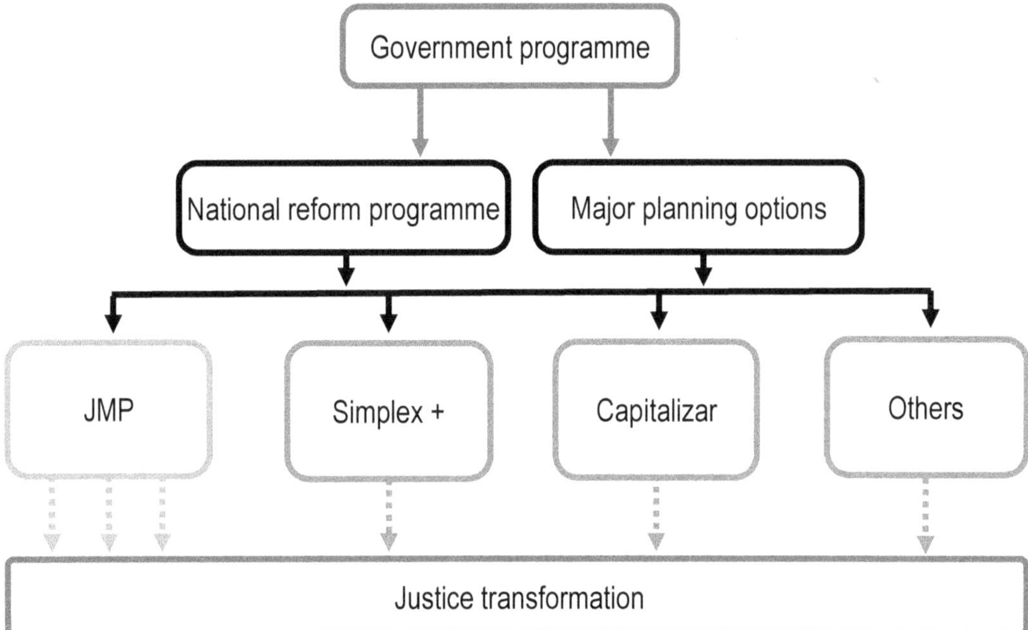

The main strategic documents regarding the government's action in the domain of justice include (Figure 2.1):

- The *Government's Programme*, which sets out the main political guidelines and measures to be developed in the various areas of governmental activity, including the domain of justice. The Programme of the XXI Government makes the commitment to render justice more agile, by assuming a management perspective with a view to modernisation, simplification and rationalisation. This commitment is structured in five different sets of concrete measures. A first set aims at: improving the management of the judicial system and comprises, for instance, the implementation of a productivity incentive scheme for courts; the development of information and communication technology (ICT) tools for court and workload management; the possibility of reallocating cases according to the "natural judge" principle;[6] and the introduction of a "Simplex philosophy" for courts. A second set of measures looks to relieve congestion in courts and focuses mainly on the reinforcement of alternative dispute resolution (ADR). A third set of measures intends to simplify and dematerialise judicial procedures and the fourth to bring justice closer to citizens, including the implementation of a new attendance service for citizens and the adoption of plain language in essential procedural acts. Finally, the government commits to measures aiming to improve the quality of the administration of justice, promoting, for instance, the training of judges and court clerks and the improvement of legal aid.[7]

- The *Major Planning Options*, which translate the government programme into concrete action, define the main strategic guidelines for the country's economic and social development policy. Every year, the government must submit to the parliament a bill establishing major planning options, together with the budget proposal. For 2019, the options include, among several others: the reinforcement of ADR (in view of developing a platform for managing pending cases in justice of the peace courts and arbitration centres); the continuous upgrade of the information systems that support courts (the administrative and fiscal courts information system SITAF and web portal Citius) with the creation of new functionalities; the development of an online Justice Digital Services Platform; the development of a Justice Hub, composed of three competency centres: i) a Security Operational Centre (for managing, monitoring and ensuring security in information systems); ii) a Digital Transformation Centre (for monitoring and developing internal procedures aiming at digital transformation); iii) a Centre for the Modernisation of Infrastructures. Once approved by the parliament, the government develops specific plans in different sectors, including justice.
- The *National Reform Programme* is also an essential element in defining a medium-term strategy to enable Portugal to launch a set of structural reforms to promote the relaunching of investment and contribute to the sustainability of public finances by 2020. Over time, integrating justice-related elements into such plans can help demonstrate its impacts on the economy, investment and business climate.

In line with good international practices (Box 2.2) and to support the implementation of a high-level vision, the current government has developed several subprogrammes, including those that apply to the justice sector (discussed further below):

- The Justiça + Próxima programme aims to develop a swift, transparent and human justice that is closer to and co-designed by citizens (see below).
- The Capitalizar programme integrates a set of 64 measures aiming to support the capitalisation of enterprises, the recovery of investment and the relaunch of the economy. The programme is divided into five pillars: i) administrative simplification and systemic framework; ii) taxation; iii) business restructuring; iv) leverage of financing and investment; and v) capital market promotion. Under the third pillar, some measures were adopted that directly involve courts, such as modifications made to the business revitalisation process. The programme specifically focuses on capitalising Portuguese enterprises by reinforcing equity and reducing their levels of indebtedness. This involves revision of the Insolvency Code, the introduction of an out-of-court Regime for Companies' Recovery, and out-of-court repossession of the collateral (pledge) legal framework, the creation of a Business Recovery Mediator Regime (a new class of professionals to help small- and medium-sized enterprises (SMEs), the strengthening of the legal regime for debt to equity swap (by giving creditors a chance to save companies with or without the equity holders' agreement), and the setting up of an Early Warning Regime and electronic proceedings for insolvency cases.
- The Simplex + programme aims to modernise public administration and was launched by the current government to further the action of the initial Simplex programme introduced in 2006 (see below).

Box 2.2. Selected examples of justice transformation efforts in OECD countries

United Kingdom – The transformation of HMCTS

HM Courts and Tribunals Service (HMCTS) launched a project in 2016 to reform the justice system and modernise courts. Completion is expected in 2023, with targets including 5 000 fewer staff, 2.4 million fewer cases, and a GBP 265 million reduction in spending. The GBP 1 billion project is expected to modernise 50 distinct programmes in the operations of criminal, family and civil matters including the incorporation of digital services, online filing and claim processing, national infrastructure, and video communications and technology support. A list of the reform programme's projects can be found on the Government of the United Kingdom website (Government of the United Kingdom, 2018a). The following principles were identified for the direction of the project:

- building in partnership
- increasing accessibility
- being proportionate and segmented
- strengthening a strong, independent and trusted justice heritage
- increasing transparency and accountability
- securing financial sustainability
- designing for 2050 – not 2018
- putting people at the heart of the system.

In 2017, the first stage of the reform was completed, seeing an increase in income generated by the estate reforms. Several challenges to the project have already been identified, however. This includes delays in developing and implementing a case management system (necessary to create full digital capabilities), a shortfall in expected funding, an extended timeline and a reduced scope of reform. The project also relies on organisations to invest in new technology while having limited control over enforcement in doing so, as well as the introduction and approval of new legislation to legitimise virtual hearings. It has been recommended that the HMCTS work with organisations in the justice system as well as the Ministry of Justice to anticipate and manage adverse consequences of the project's implementation and to address the challenges above.

New Zealand – Improving people's experience

New Zealand's modernisation of the courts project was launched in 2013 and the following goals were defined (New Zealand Ministry of Justice, 2018a):

- reduce the time it takes to hear and resolve matters in a court or tribunal
- improve the experience of court users
- simplify and standardise processes to improve productivity and efficiency
- reduce dependency on physical locations.

The project is anticipated to be completed in 2022. It includes electronic self-service, case flow management, event management, remote participation, and business intelligence and performance to deliver a more citizen-centric provision of services and enhance access to justice. In conjunction with these deliverables, the Ministry of Justice seeks to implement two bills – the Court Matters Bill and the Tribunals Powers and Procedures Legislation Bill, to provide the legal framework necessary for the change (New Zealand Ministry of Justice, 2018b):

Sources: Government of the United Kingdom (2018a), *The HMCTS Reform Programme*, https://www.gov.uk/guidance/the-hmcts-reform-programme; Morse, A. (2018), "Early progress in transforming courts and tribunals", https://www.nao.org.uk/press-release/early-progress-in-transforming-courts-and-tribunals/; Government of the United Kingdom (2018b), *HMCTS Reform Programme Projects Explained*, https://www.gov.uk/guidance/hmcts-reform-programme-projects-explained; Acland-Hood, S. (2018), "Modernising the Courts and Tribunals Service", https://www.ucl.ac.uk/laws/sites/laws/files/ucl_foj_01_03_acland-hood.pdf; Controller and Auditor General (2017), *Ministry of Justice: Modernising Court Services*, https://www.oag.govt.nz/2017/courts/docs/courts.pdf; New Zealand Ministry of Justice (2018a), *Modernising Courts and Tribunals*, https://www.justice.govt.nz/about/about-us/our-strategy/modernising-courts-and-tribunals/; New Zealand Ministry of Justice (2018b), *Statement of Intent*, https://www.justice.govt.nz/assets/Documents/Publications/Ministry-of-Justice-statement-of-intent-2017-to-2022.pdf.

The Justiça + Próxima programme

The Justiça + Próxima programme spans the entire 2015-19 legislature and aims to increase transparency and trust in the justice institutions acting through four fundamental pillars (Ministry of Justice of Portugal, 2016):

- enhancing efficiency and strengthening justice sector management through simplification and dematerialisation of procedures and the use of interoperable technologies
- innovation, by modernising justice
- proximity, pursuing the citizen-centric approach, by offering clear, transparent and accountable information
- humanisation, by valuing tangible and intangible resources.

Justiça + Próxima is, thus, composed of multiple initiatives (Box 2.3), some of which were proposed by citizens and justice stakeholders, with the technology used to provide for such targets by promoting a "digital by default" principle for courts and other justice stakeholders. In part, Justiça + Próxima also contributes to the Simplex + programme.[8]

Box 2.3. Selected measures of the Justiça + Próxima programme

Alternative dispute resolution (ADR)

- Electronic information on alternative means of dispute resolution.
- Reassessment of the business model of peace courts and reorganisation and streamlining of the network of justices of the peace.
- Network boosting consumer conflict arbitration centres.

Collaboration

- Justice for All of Us and Justice Forum.
- Court +.
- System management indicators of courts.
- Management information system of courts of first instance.

Courts digital transformation

- Citius web portal (e.g. remote access by magistrates, alert service, SISAAE interface [computer support system for enforcement officers activity], faster preparation of the final procedure account, liaison with GNR (National Republican Guard), inventory and review of available forms, access by insolvency administrators).

- Access by enforcement officers linked to enforcement proceedings.
- Wi-Fi in courts and rollout of attendance model, courtroom management system, My Court system and automatic transcription.
- Renewal and strengthening of computer equipment and management tools, and productivity of the courts.
- One-stop-shop in administrative and tax courts.
- Inclusion of debtors in the public list of debtors under PEPEX (pre-judicial extrajudicial procedure).
- SICRIM (online criminal register portal), integration into the European system, criminal records online and legal electronic certificate.
- Code of Procedure in Administrative Courts/SITAF (administrative and fiscal courts information system) (e.g. mandatory e-submission of procedural documents, electronic interface, automatic notifications).
- Online portal registration and automatic access management for agents and court administrators, online consultation on the status of cases.

Forensic medicine

- Improved management, service system, operational capacity and process control in INMLCF (National Institute of Forensic Medicine and Forensic Sciences).

Industrial property

- Granting orders of trademarks, design and patents.
- INPI (National Industrial Property Institute) network.

Infrastructure

- Installing a central disaster recovery.
- Strengthening security and application data of justice's information systems.

Innovation

- Creation of space for justice innovation.
- Paperless processes for State Secretary of Justice.

Justice portal

- Digital justice platform and digital service area in courts.
- Online claim service with the Citizen Card.

Knowledge management

- Digital document repository.

Language simplification

- Improved communication with citizens on payment orders.

Attorney-General's Office

- Prosecutor in Action programme.

Judicial police

- Management system for forensic laboratory activity.
- Cyber intelligence and online justice.
- International police co-operation: Passenger Information Unit (PIU).
- Strengthening the capacity of the Forensic Expertise system.
- Enhancing the capacity to collect and analyse digital evidence by the judicial police.
- Creation of "malware" incubators for analysis and research purposes.
- Acquisition of Wi-Fi – Man in the Middle (MITM) technology solution.

Registries

- Automation of birth, death, will, land and other registries.
- Modernisation of platforms and introduction of new services in registries and notaries.

Resolve Court

- Resolve Court, a pilot court that offers justice and other social services (in partnership with civil society and public administration) with a view to bringing together the judicial function and the resolution of social, economic and labour problems at the local and regional levels.

Transparency

- Strategic "Open Government" in court plan

Source: Ministry of Justice of Portugal, 2019.

The result is a comprehensive digitalisation and modernisation package consisting of more than 175 measures (new measures are continuously added to the plan),[9] with a total budget of EUR 44 million. These measures are continuously adjusted through an online public consultation process on a dedicated website: www.justicamaisproxima.mj.pt. Each of the initiatives identifies various details on the necessary changes and expected impacts, including the number of targeted/affected companies and estimated savings. The plan specifically targets the needs of various stakeholders of the justice system, including citizens, courts, Ministry of Justice, lawyers, solicitors and others (Table 2.1).

Table 2.1. A justice transformation focused on people and businesses

Improving services, simplifying processes and innovating in courts following "digital by default" while focusing on citizens and businesses

Courts	• Management Indicators System • Legal fees payment status' automated verification and registry • Automated production and expedition of postal notifications • Modernisation of core IT systems • Promotion of a "continuous improvement" mindset • Dematerialised fingerprints' communication • Automatic media transcription • Automated judicial processes' bill calc. • Activities and team management electronic functionalities	• Alert service about diligences changes • Electronic judicial certificate • Electronic notifications • Mandatory electronic submission and access to judicial processes • Real-time verification of legal status during authentication • New digital services portal for admin\fiscal courts • Mandatory report obligations and access to public databases for insolvency practitioners and improved supervision tools	**Lawyers, solicitors, insolvency administration,** ...

Ministry of Justice	• Changes to the Organisation of the Judiciary System • Administrative\fiscal courts official statistics • One-Stop-Shop for administrative\fiscal courts • Mandatory electronic processing (all courts) • Strategic Plan for Information Systems • Resource planning and management systems for courts administration • Improved redundancy and reinforcement of technical infrastructures • Electronic Interoperability with external entities (Health, Social Security, Education, European Case Law Identifier.	• Aggregated\centralised directory of digital services • Electronic criminal record certificate • Temporary digital authentication methods • Electronic judicial certificate • Language simplification of notifications • Online to processes in courts • Reformulation of Citizens' frontend service inside courts • Official statistics portal's modernisation with interactive tools • Improving perceptions of what really depends on courts • Operational courts and systems' "transparency" indicators	**Citizens and businesses**

Source: Ministry of Justice of Portugal, 2019.

The process for identifying measures, included as part of the Justiça + Próxima programme, represents an innovative, collaborative and bottom-up effort, with significant input from stakeholders within the judiciary, such as practising judges, the High Council for the Administrative and Fiscal Courts and the High Council of the Judiciary. This consultation process involves a series of workshops in which participants are asked to propose initiatives, including their potential impact.

The design of the plan also engages people and businesses using ICT platforms and allows every stakeholder to submit an idea for the improvement of the justice system, providing an opportunity to make governance and service delivery more collaborative, participatory and transparent. By establishing such procedures for service delivery, justice sectors and governments at large, these actors will become more interconnected and enhance co-operation with internal and external stakeholders.

More broadly, these strategies are also connected to the country's broader service modernisation agendas, including Portugal's ICT Strategy 2020 (Government of Portugal, 2018).

All these strategies are strongly interlinked and represent a broad vision of the Portuguese government for delivering services that are user-driven and respond to citizen needs, including faster and more responsive dispute resolution and increased trust in justice, with a view to fostering inclusive growth.

In parallel, in the criminal justice domain and in accordance with the Framework Law on Criminal Policy, the government submits to parliament a bill establishing criminal policy goals, priorities and guidelines every two years.[10] The policy requires consultation with a wide range of stakeholders, including the High Council of the Judiciary, the High Council for the Public Prosecution, the Coordinating Council of the Criminal Police Bodies, the High Council of Internal Security, the Security Coordinating Office and the Portuguese Bar Association.

These strategies present important elements of the vision to enhance efficiency, transparency, user-centricity and effectiveness of the Portuguese justice sector. They are linked to the overall government vision, which provides solid anchoring in the country's development priorities. Looking ahead and building on this solid foundation, Portugal may consider developing a longer-term justice strategy which brings together different branches of power, goes beyond the electoral cycle and integrates the needs of the people who may be currently excluded from the justice system, with little or no access to court or legal assistance.

Towards a simpler, digital, open and innovative justice system

Building on these strategies, the specific modernisation initiatives in Portugal's justice sector are developed through three main pillars:

Pillar 1. Simplification

Simplification efforts in the justice sector are primarily developed through the Simplex + programme. Launched in 2016, Simplex + is a cross-cutting programme composed of a set of measures that aims to ensure the simplification of administrative and legislative processes in order to facilitate citizen and business interaction with the administration. Similar to its predecessors, the programme contributes to increasing the internal efficiency of the public services leading to shorter response times to citizen and business requests made to public authorities. Selected justice-related measures developed through Simplex + include (Box 2.4):

- Interoperability of information through dematerialisation of data support and introduction of e-channels between courts, other justice institutions and other entities in the social security, health, education and security sectors.
- An online certificate for legal entities to enable fast delivery.
- The simplification of court fee payment, waving the need to join paper-based documents certifying payment.
- The development of a judicial costs simulator, the possibility of requesting criminal record certificates online, by authenticating with the Citizen Card or the Digital Mobile Key, made available on the portal once the fee has been paid (Ministry of Justice of Portugal, n.d.).
- The implementation of electronic proceedings between tax administration and administrative and fiscal courts.
- User-subscribed SMS or email alerts for the renewal of citizen cards, driver's licenses, passports, or online certificates for legal entities.
- Online consultation by citizens of their judicial cases.
- The simplification of court notifications and writs of summons, ensuring they are legally accurate and comprehensible for citizens, etc.

The underlying objectives of these efforts include improvements to public sector efficiency and effectiveness, support for the development of the business climate and collecting data from citizens and businesses following the "once only" principle. The main aim of these efforts was to identify and target concrete problems in different sectors of the economy.

The project was designed to meet the needs of public service users, thus putting people and businesses at the centre by consulting them during the programme's design and implementation. The consultation method aimed to integrate the inputs of various stakeholders. In addition to workshops held throughout the country with citizens and businesses, the Simplex + website offered citizens the possibility of presenting innovative ideas to be evaluated for inclusion in the project. In 2017, aiming at further participation of public administration staff, Simplex Jam was introduced as a methodology to generate new ideas for improving public services by creating joint teams from different public administration departments. Simplex + builds on an original bottom-up approach in which rationalisation opportunities were identified through public consultations (see below).[11]

Box 2.4. Examples of Simplex + achievements in the justice sector

- The introduction of the Simplex philosophy in court, in internal and external communication practices with citizens, organisations and judicial activity support functions.
- The introduction of online certificates for legal entities to enable fast delivery.
- The simplification of court fee payments, waving the need to enclose paper-based documents certifying payment.
- The development of a judicial costs simulator.
- Improved social security registry management.
- The implementation and strengthening of the consumer arbitration network, which aims to promote the extrajudicial resolution of conflicts between consumer and companies.
- No further need to provide proof of payment for legal fees and other costs during the judicial procedures.
- The creation of a single appointment service for booking various registration services online.
- A new mobile application for pilot courts to inform users about the status of legal steps and timelines.
- Online criminal record requests, with authentication via the Citizen Card or Digital Mobile Key, made available on the portal once the fee has been paid.
- The implementation of electronic proceedings between tax administration and administrative and fiscal courts.
- Online consultation by citizens of their judicial cases.
- The simplification of court notifications and writs of summons, ensuring they are legally accurate and comprehensible for citizens.
- The creation of an SMS alert system for lawyers informing them of adjourned hearings.

Source: Ministry of Justice of Portugal, 2019.

Simplex + has introduced a charter of principles, some of which included:

1. Public administration affairs immediately processed and followed up at a single point of contact for citizens and businesses.
2. Public services accessed online or at a nearby counter.
3. Availability of documents online.
4. Information given to public administration following the "once only" principle.
5. Easy access to public information.
6. Online authentication in a safe and user-friendly manner.
7. Services scheduled online.

More recently, Simplex + activities are being structured according to different life events: birth, health, education, vehicles, work, business, home, family, retirement and death, with three transversal events, leisure, lifelong events and more efficient public administration.

According to Portuguese officials, Simplex initiatives have also been undergoing detailed assessment in relation to their implementation and delivery of results (see section on evaluation and monitoring).

Moreover, simplification measures extend beyond the Simplex + programme. Thus, as part of the Justiça + Próxima programme, parties are now exempt from sending proof of court fee payments to the court, as they are automatically validated by a specific code (*Documento Único de Cobrança*), making for more automation and thereby reducing the number of documents to be added to the pleading. This innovation also leads to the simplification of the preparation of the final liquidation of court fees of the judicial case.

Pillar 2. Digital solutions

Similar to other government services, justice systems in many places around the world have begun to use digital tools. As part of the Justiça + Próxima programme, Portugal is increasingly employing IT applications in the justice system, including for case management, e-filing, document management, digitalisation of courtroom functions, human resources management (HRM) tools, help desk and public information systems, in order to facilitate the accessibility of justice, especially in courthouses. The current efforts – led by a range of stakeholders across public institutions (Box 2.5) – can be presented as follows:

- *Digitalisation (dematerialisation) of case management and information* – Dematerialisation of cases aims to make the relevant documents easily accessible to different users, with the option to read and annotate as appropriate. Over the past decade, Portugal has been investing in the dematerialisation of case management and information, including the Citius electronic platform, which seeks to provide a single online solution for judges, public prosecutors, lawyers, solicitors, enforcement agents and insolvency practitioners. Citius involves the modernisation of core IT systems in the courts, including judicial electronic processes from courts of first instance to the Supreme Court and more than 100 technological features in all magistrate information systems. A similar platform (SITAF) has been developed in the administrative and fiscal jurisdiction, introducing digital transmission of tax proceedings from administration to administrative and fiscal courts, an innovative feature. The introduction of the digital case file in Portugal facilitates streamlined processes, improves their quality (by reducing manual work) and reduces the costs related to production and storage of files. The adoption of SITAF would bring Portugal closer to paperless working, which can be strengthened once all courts are equipped with the relevant technologies. Combined with the process of rethinking and streamlining procedures (also as part of Simplex +), these measures have the potential to improve the speed of case processing and thus enhance both efficiency and access to justice for people.
- *Online platforms* – The new digital e-services platform www.Justica.gov.pt provides an integrated platform for all sites and eServices of justice, including cost simulators for different proceedings as well as 120 datasets of statistical information. In addition, since November 2018, all cases are accessible to parties and authorised persons through www.Tribunais.org.pt. The authorities have also introduced a range of initiatives to strengthen communication with external stakeholders, including a newsletter, a direct channel for submitting ideas and the requirement for authorities to provide feedback.

  Access to information and communication – Portugal has been taking active steps to improve access to information and communication by key stakeholders. Since 2017, parties have the possibility to consult their cases pending before judicial, administrative and fiscal courts, including enforcement cases. Moreover, the launch of a new online portal and the enforcement of the use of Citius for lawyers have enabled the courts to send writs of notice electronically, contributing to easier access to information. Lawyers should also be able to upload videos and audio to their case files, as well as receive notifications by email or text message in the event of postponement of a case hearing. It is also anticipated that citizens should be able to consult their online (from any location using electronic authentication on a web portal).

Box 2.5. Entities involved in the digitalisation process of the judicial system

The judiciary digitalisation process is carried out by the Ministry of Justice in co-operation with three other agencies. First, the Institute of Financial Management and Justice Equipment (IGFEJ) is responsible for the execution and maintenance of the technological resources and justice information systems, adapting management and professional processes to the needs of their users. It guarantees the system's security, operability and standardisation methods and procedures. Second, the definition of organisation and management policies in courts and the management and training of judicial officers are conducted by both the Directorate-General for the Administration of Justice (DGAJ) and the IGFEJ. Finally, the development, implementation and operation of information systems, as well as the ICT sessions for judges and prosecutors are covered by the Directorate-General for Justice Policy (DGPJ) in close collaboration with the IGFEJ.

The High Council of the Judiciary, the High Council for the Administrative and Fiscal Courts, the Attorney-General Office, the Board for Monitoring Peace Courts and the DGPJ jointly manage data proceedings. These institutions also have an important consultative role for the Co-ordinating Commission for the Management of Data Relating to the Judicial System. Such a commission, created by means of Law no. 34/2009, also: guarantees co-ordination among the entities in charge of the management of judicial data; promotes and monitors system security audits; establishes the security requirements of the system; creates and maintains an updated record of the technicians who process that data; and reports any violation of the data legal regime related to the judicial system for criminal or disciplinary proceedings.

The Portuguese Bar Association also plays an important role in the process of justice digitalisation. This entity provides its associates with the digital signature needed to access Citius and the national information system that integrates Citius to provide information on lawyers' professional data and their legal assistance intervention.

Similarly, the Association of Prosecutors and Enforcement Officials (OSAE) has developed a software solution called GPESE/SISAAE (Public Office Procedural Management Guidelines for Civil Servants) which also articulates with the Citius system.

Last but not least, the Commission for Monitoring Court Assistants, created by Law no. 77/2013, monitors, inspects and determines disciplinary measures for assistants in courts, and uses Citius and SISAAE to pursue dematerialisation and electronic procedures in Courts to strength transparency, swiftness and efficiency of all judicial actors involved in enforcement and insolvency procedures.

Source: Government of Portugal Official website.

Importantly, in line with the philosophy of Simplex +, the Justiça + Próxima programme includes initiatives on clear language and information aimed at citizens, including the pilot "writing clear" in judicial processes. In particular, Portugal has introduced rules and norms for presenting judgments and listing the grounds given by the judge. For example, it has implemented "standardised" judicial documents, which aim to make it easier for judges to draft decisions and for litigants to understand them (Ministry of Justice of Portugal, 2017) (Figure 2.2).

Figure 2.2. Payment order template

Before

Balcão Nacional de Injunções

NOTIFICAÇÃO

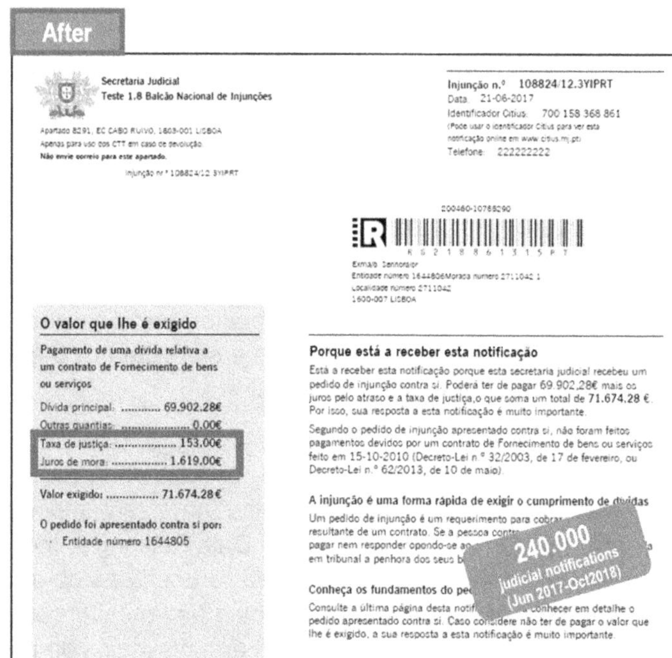

After

Secretaria Judicial
Teste 1.8 Balcão Nacional de Injunções

Apartado 8291, EC CABO RUIVO, 1803-001 LISBOA
Apenas para uso dos CTT em caso de devolução.
Não envie correio para este apartado.

Injunção nº 108824/12.3YIPRT

Injunção n.º 108824/12.3YIPRT
Data: 21-06-2017
Identificador Citius: 700 158 368 861
(Pode usar o identificador Citius para ver esta notificação online em www.citius.mj.pt)
Telefone: 222222222

1600-007 LISBOA

O valor que lhe é exigido

Pagamento de uma dívida relativa a um contrato de Fornecimento de bens ou serviços

Dívida principal: .... 69.902.28€
Outras quantias: .... 0.00€
Taxa de justiça: .... 153.00€
Juros de mora: .... 1.619.00€

Valor exigido: .... 71.674.28€

O pedido foi apresentado contra si por:
Entidade número 1644805

Porque está a receber esta notificação

Está a receber esta notificação porque esta secretaria judicial recebeu um pedido de injunção contra si. Poderá ter de pagar 69.902,28€ mais os juros pelo atraso e a taxa de justiça, o que soma um total de **71.674.28 €**. Por isso, sua resposta a esta notificação é muito importante.

Segundo o pedido de injunção apresentado contra si, não foram feitos pagamentos devidos por um contrato de Fornecimento de bens ou serviços feito em 15-10-2010 (Decreto-Lei n.º 32/2003, de 17 de fevereiro, ou Decreto-Lei n.º 62/2013, de 10 de maio).

A injunção é uma forma rápida de exigir o cumprimento de dívidas

Um pedido de injunção é um requerimento para cobrar ... resultante de um contrato. Se a pessoa ... pagar nem responder opondo-se ao ... em tribunal a penhora dos seus b...

Conheça os fundamentos do pe...

Consulte a última página desta notif... conhecer em detalhe o pedido apresentado contra si. Caso considere não ter de pagar o valor que lhe é exigido, a sua resposta a esta notificação é muito importante.

Source: Ministry of Justice of Portugal, 2019.

The introduction of these tools also aims to help the country and its courts, non-judicial mechanisms and legal aid/assistance to face current pressure on available resources effectively. It can support courts in fulfilling their fundamental mission for society by providing justice for all, an objective mirrored in UN Sustainable Development Goal (SDG) target 16.3, to which Portugal has committed under the 2030 Agenda for Sustainable Development. Indeed, Portugal has obtained increasingly significant scores in all areas of integration of technology in court operations – defined by the European Commission for the Efficiency of Justice (CEPEJ) as the direct assistance to judges and court clerks, support for court administration and management, and support for interaction/communication between courts and parties – since 2010.[12] In fact, Portugal is considered as one of the most advanced countries in Europe in terms of digitalisation in the justice sector (CEPEJ, 2018).

Current transformation efforts in Portugal provide a strong foundation to further mobilise technological capabilities, through emerging technologies (such as artificial intelligence and blockchain) to build a digitally-enabled, seamless, people-centred justice ecosystem. In line with good practices increasingly found in OECD countries, such an ecosystem could integrate both judicial and alternative mechanisms to resolve disputes, support effective triage of cases and enable multichannel dispute resolution avenues.

Portugal is currently preparing a basis for establishing online systems that could support the resolution of disputes. These systems could help diagnose the legal problems of citizens and businesses, and inform them of their rights and options in order to help protect them and resolve their disputes by using big data. They can also provide an assisted negotiation stage, which could be followed by a seamless transition to an adjudication, depending on the nature of the dispute and involved stakeholders. This type of one-stop-shop for dispute resolution can facilitate the creation of a justice ecosystem and transform the resolution of disputes (Taskforce on Justice, 2019).

To take the "one-stop justice shop" further, the initiative is scheduled to be linked to the existing citizens' portal to facilitate early identification of problems and provide a unique interface for citizens. Interoperability of data and big data could also help in this regard. The single digital Citizen Card and recently introduced

Digital Mobile Key in Portugal could be extended to legal and justice services to enable greater accessibility of such services and shift their focus on the preventive and restorative facets.

In addition, in order to maximise the impact of transformation efforts and enable judges to focus more on the adjudication of complex cases (which require a certain level of scrutiny and consideration), Portugal may consider developing a holistic service delivery system that integrates alternative dispute resolution (ADR) mechanisms to ensure that courts do not consider unnecessary cases. Portugal, like other OECD countries, has already adopted a number of important initiatives in this regard, by establishing common and integrated online platforms for different ADR channels, and planning the integration with the court platform (Box 2.6). This would serve as a strong basis for developing an integrated triage system for resolving disputes.

Box 2.6. Online dispute resolution

Online dispute resolution (ODR) is an electronic form of dispute resolution. It can take the format of negotiation, mediation or arbitration and utilises technology to facilitate communication and document sharing between parties. ODR can increase access to justice for those living in a remote location and can provide a quicker and simpler route to dispute resolution. Internationally, ODR initiatives have been primarily launched for consumer complaints, small civil claims and financial family law matters. The 2013 Directive on ADR for Consumer Disputes and the 2013 Regulation on ODR for Consumer Disputes have made online dispute resolution a priority in the European Union.

Canada – The Canadian Civil Resolution Tribunal

The Civil Resolution Tribunal was established in 2012 under the Civil Resolution Tribunal Act. It started with condominium disputes in 2016 and began resolving small claims in 2017. The goal is to encourage collaborative problem-solving approaches to dispute resolution. Small tribunal claims must go through the tribunal before proceeding to provincial court. However, the court still has a role if the tribunal refuses to resolve the claim, a party objects to the tribunal's decision, or if it is determined that the tribunal does not have jurisdiction. This is Canada's first online tribunal. It is available for small claims disputes dealing with debts, damages and recovery of personal property of CAD 5 000 and under, or condominium property disputes of any value. The tribunal is expected to roll out capacity to deal with motor vehicle accident claims of CAD 50 000 and under starting April 2019. Individuals use the Solution Explorer to diagnose their dispute and obtain free legal information and standard templates. If they cannot resolve the dispute, they can apply directly from this software using a type form. Once the application is accepted, a secure and confidential negotiation platform is provided for the parties to attempt to reach an agreement. If an agreement cannot be reached, a facilitator will be appointed to aid the parties. At this stage, any agreement made can be turned into an order which can be enforced as though it was a court order. If a decision still cannot be reached, an independent member of the tribunal will make a decision – again, which can be enforced like a court order. The tribunal is part of the justice system and has independent and neutral members. Fees are charged to file a dispute based on the amount in the claim. If individuals do not have access to a computer, they can also complete the application on paper.

Canada – MyLawBC

This is another online platform for those going through a separation. It offers three pathways – drafting a separation plan, obtaining a family order and serving a court document. Each pathway asks the user questions and leads them to a list of steps of what to do next. It also acts as a negotiation platform for spouses to discuss issues and draft an agreement simultaneously. Each of the pathways takes 20 minutes or less to complete. The platform also has a dialogue tool, which builds the framework of a legal agreement for the parties to complete. The soft launch took place in February 2016 on family law issues and the project expanded to include foreclosure matters in March 2016. Changes were rolled out in the following months and developers are making adjustments based on public interaction with the site.

England and Wales – Online claims system pilot

Claims of up to GBP 10 000 can be made and the platform provides online dispute resolution and mediation. Operational since 2017, it has been developed in consultation with the judiciary, representatives from the advice and legal community as well as users.

The Netherlands – Rechtwijer 2.0 and Justice42

The Rechtwijer 2.0 platform was available for divorce and separation proceedings and rolled out in two versions. The first version gave the user an interactive experience tailored to their needs with advice and referrals. The second sought to provide online dispute resolution. The project was part of a three-year collaboration between the Hague Institute for Innovation of Law (HiiL), the Dutch Legal Aid Board and Modria. It was dissolved in July 2017 as it became financially unsustainable for the private sector but was transformed into Justice42. Justice42 focuses primarily on the Dutch divorce market and seeks to incorporate the lessons learned from Rechtwijer. Lessons learned from Rechtwijer include:

- users not wanting to fund solutions themselves
- dwindling public subsidy for the project making private funding a requirement
- only 1% of divorces handled in the Netherlands.

After looking at the lessons learned above, Justice42 was designed as an online platform to aid couples in divorce agreements. It allows the entire divorce to be arranged online, at a fixed price per stage and with guidance, using the platform www.uitelkaar.nl.

United States – Teleservices

Drug courts in Montana are using teleservices to help those in remote areas. The services can perform a remote screening and referral process for cases, allow individuals to observe video proceedings remotely and enable videoconferencing for regular status hearings or one-on-one counselling. The courts are also using an application to monitor alcohol use and location and can connect a breathalyser device to the user's phone with an alert or timer indicating when this must be used. In addition, text messages for motivational support, reminders and community events are sent to the individual.

Source: Civil Resolution Tribunal (2019), *Welcome to the Civil Resolution Tribunal*, http://civilresolutionbc.ca; British Columbia Legal Services Society (2016), *MyLawBC*, http://factum.mylawbc.com/blog; My Law BC (2019), *Separation, Divorce and Family Matters*, https://mylawbc.com/; Government of the United Kingdom (2018c), "Quicker way to resolve claim disputes launched online", www.gov.uk/government/news/quicker-way-to-resolve-claim-disputes-launched-online; Committee for Justice (2016), "Report on justice in the 21st century: Innovative approaches for the criminal justice system in Northern Ireland", www.niassembly.gov.uk/globalassets/documents/justice-2011-2016/copy-of-the-justice-in-the-21st-century-report-with-appendices.pdf; Justice42 (2017), *Homepage*, http://justice42.nl (accessed 18 February 2019); Otis, K. et al. (2017), *Teleservices: Happening Now!*, www.courtinnovation.org/sites/default/files/documents/Teleservices.pdf.

Finally, in view of the broader strategic objective of Portugal to facilitate sound business climate and user-centricity, there is scope to link legal services and dispute resolution for businesses to the online business portal. To be effective, these efforts should be underpinned by a systematic survey of business legal needs, experiences and barriers in resolving disputes in order to help Portugal to tailor further its initiatives and services, supporting efficient dispute resolution for an effective business climate.

Pillar 3. Fostering justice innovation

Justice innovation can play an important role in boosting productivity and citizen responsiveness as well as finding solutions to complex problems. Portugal is investing special efforts to promote a culture of innovation to transform the nature of service delivery and identify new solutions to complex challenges, such as promoting social and territorial cohesion. One example is a property one-stop-shop pilot project tested in 14 municipalities. After significant fires affected the Portuguese territory in 2018, the authorities recognised the lack of information about landowners and property boundaries, also affecting other areas of governance, such as finance (taxation), agriculture and the environment. To address these gaps, the authorities have created an electronic platform linking owners and public administration in order to provide, through interoperability, a one-stop shop to access the integrated information of several public entities and to promote property identification and facilitated data modification. A deductive model was first created, listing properties and land according to information available in different public administration databases, both central and local (Box 2.7). The model allowed the development of an algorithm capable of identifying new properties and their characteristics.

Box 2.7. The *Balcão Único do Prédio* (BUPi, Property One-stop Shop) project

The Portuguese government piloted the BUPi (*Balcão Único do Prédio*, One-stop Shop for Properties) project to better identify land, its owners and boundaries for increased protection and territorial planning. This initiative aimed to create incentives for owners to identify their land and was designed as a collaborative platform with interoperating data available from central and local authorities.

The project was designed for a better understanding of the territory, its landowners and property boundaries, to better protect them and to improve land-use planning. It is a collaborative initiative involving different government areas: justice (registries), environment, agriculture, finances as well as municipalities.

To begin with, ten municipalities were selected to participate and test a pilot version of the project, for which the first conclusions and findings would be validated a year later and, after that, implemented on a national scale. The project involved developing a closer, decentralised customer service experience, made up of both mobile and physical information counters, tailored to the citizens' requirements. The information gathered during the pilot is accessible, interoperable and available on a single platform, allowing data to be filed, organised and accessed in a simple, visual and user-friendly way. After, harnessing existing knowledge of the territory, divided up among different public and non-public databases, the authorities developed an algorithm capable of identifying new properties, estimating their locations, sizes, shapes and owners. Pilot testing led to automated determination of probable location, allowing for an accelerated process.

Some of the success factors included:

- Government commitment both on a national and regional scale with the necessary resources (financial, team allocation with empowerment and autonomy).
- Development and availability of the necessary tools to design the processes, in particular for the municipalities, registries and other organisations.
- Clear and active involvement of local associations and companies for a broader and more effective adoption of land identification and location.
- Fast and clear communication among those involved, in particular to clarify doubts on or improve the BUPi project.

- Maturity of technologies and their ease of use, agility and adaptability of processes and, above all, the active and continuous involvement of stakeholders.
- Structured team of procedural and technological platform support.
- Availability of mapping and big data analysis to provide and improve the location of properties.

Source: Ministry of Justice of Portugal, 2019.

In parallel, to foster further the spirit of innovation in the justice sector, the authorities are adopting modern tools, such as the establishment of the Justice Innovation Hub (Box 2.8). In addition, the Ministry of Justice introduced new ways of working in a more collaborative environment by creating an innovation room as a place to hold brainstorming sessions, discussions and workshops.

Box 2.8. Justice Innovation Hub in Portugal

The Justice Hub is a collaborative workspace created at the Justice Campus in Lisbon and aims to aggregate teams involved in justice modernisation and transformation projects.

This is a project-oriented work model, with multidisciplinary teams from different entities within the justice system as well as external, involving project managers, designers, development teams, working in a single space on different projects, from transformation initiatives, such as the new registry model, to modernisation, such as Simplified Land Registration, BUPi, SIRAUTO, the Digital Justice Platform and various associated services, including certificates or even the different Citius interfaces.

Different events linked to good practices, such as workshops, community initiatives and hackathons, will also be developed in this space. The space aims to serve as a collaborative model between the different areas of public administration, but also in interaction with start-ups and universities in order to facilitate value and knowledge transfer to the administration of justice.

Source: Government of Portugal, 2019.

The ministry also reports implementing agile methodologies to introduce change and question the status quo whenever possible, with a view to enhancing flexibility and efficiency in managing resources, contributing to a more productive work environment and setting up efficient communication channels between the parties involved. In particular, it reports using different management improvement techniques (e.g. Kaizen) in courts in order to promote continuous improvement and to stimulate a new environment and culture among the courts and clerks.

Optimising justice service delivery

Judicial map

The location of courts directly affects the distance citizens must travel for justice, the judicial caseload and potential backlog, the public monies required to staff or resource courts, and the quality and performance of services. A properly drawn judicial map can optimise case flow and improve co-ordination between judges at different offices. Reforming the judicial map calls for an understanding of how litigation is distributed in terms of volume, type and proximity and the efficiencies or shortcomings in court performance and its users. In particular, by using an overview of the current map and case flow, a list of court objectives and measurable performance indicators, one can ensure a judicial map operates effectively and provides equal access to justice (CEPEJ, 2013) (Box 2.9).

The structure of the judicial map has undergone multiple reforms over the last years in Portugal, including the 2013 reform, which consolidated the country's 231 judicial courts of first instance into 23 district clusters. In this context, the Justiça + Próxima programme, in turn, envisages a series of measures to further optimise the judicial map, which aim to alleviate some concerns about the growing concentration and centralisation of courts, in view of the distance between the courts and some population living in remote areas. In particular, authorities report re-evaluating the judicial map,[13] reopening several small courts[14] and strengthening court capacities for video conferencing[15] and other equipment.

Furthermore, in order to improve court infrastructure to accommodate the reforms – among other initiatives[16] – Portugal has introduced a Strategic Multi-Year 2018-28 Plan for Improvement and Modernisation of Courts, which was developed through a series of public discussions and includes measures to strengthen physical infrastructure, human resources and the use of technology in courts.[17]

Finally, in response to concerns about the resulting discontinuity in data at court district level (OECD, 2019), the Portuguese authorities report that most of the data was recovered and data collection resumed in late 2015/early 2016 after a series of consistency tests.

It would be important to evaluate the impacts of these initiatives on the accessibility of justice services, quality of justice infrastructure and data collection processes.

Court specialisation

The experience of OECD member states shows that specialised courts can enhance the timeliness and improve the quality of justice services (Box 2.10). These courts provide dedicated services to deal with technical or community-related matters and are often used to improve efficiency by allowing judges to deepen knowledge in specific areas of law, reducing judicial workloads in general courts of first instance and providing a consistent and accurate interpretation of the law.

In Portugal, the 2013 Law on Judicial Organisation placed an emphasis on various types of specialisation, introducing a new model of competencies (specialised courts and divisions in all territory, not only in urban centres). The grouping in clusters has allowed greater specialisation of courts. Notably, specialisation was in many instances achieved through specialised "local sections or branches" (e.g. commercial courts are not standalone courts but branches within a district court; thus, 16 courts specialising in commercial cases compared to the 4 prior to the reform, are all local sections or branches). Authorities report that the number of labour sections has also increased and they now cover 70% of the territory (a significant increase from 20%). Overall, the reform also increased the number of family and juvenile courts, criminal instruction courts, enforcement courts and commercial courts. To serve in specialised courts, judges should have at least ten years of experience.[18] Greater investment in specialised judicial training could further help to maximise the effectiveness of these reforms (OECD, 2019).

Another important dimension of judicial specialisation is enabling judges to focus on adjudication and to limit auxiliary tasks (such as case preparation and management, research and drafting of administrative documents). As shown in the 2019 OECD Economic Survey of Portugal, evidence from OECD countries and Portugal indeed shows that judicial decision-making can significantly speed up if judges are supported by legal assistants/clerks (OECD, 2019), which is currently limited in Portugal.

Box 2.9. OECD country examples of judicial mapping for an optimised workload

France – Judicial Map reform

France underwent reform of its judicial map in 2012. During the reassessment, it was identified that 169 of the small jurisdiction courts were operating at a non-optimal level of organisation without full-time staff. This contributed to losses in performance, efficiency and the rationalisation of financial resources. In response, the judicial map was redefined and the number of jurisdictions was decreased from 1 190 to 863. In addition to jurisdictional changes, specialised courts were established for organised crime, health, terrorism and other highly technical fields. While reform to the judicial map increased the activity of the courts, this was expected given that the number of courts had decreased. It was also noted that in some jurisdictions where courts of first instance were combined, judges closely collaborate resulting in unified methods. In other jurisdictions, such as Dunkirk, the remaining court created a new specialised chamber (in this case for family matters), which decreased processing times to a lower level than the national average.

The Netherlands – Act on the Reform of the Judicial Map

The Netherlands reformed its judicial map in 2013 based on data gathered in 2010. During the assessment, it was noted that some courts were too small to handle a caseload efficiently and in a cost-effective manner while ensuring quality performance. In light of these concerns, the judicial map was redrawn to reduce the number of smaller courts, resulting in a reduction of district courts from 19 to 11, and first instance venues from 52 to 32. Merging these jurisdictions resulted in regional co-operation and lessened workload problems. The number of court boards also decreased, making court administration more efficient and effective; it was, however, noted that future thought should be given to avoid making these boards over-bureaucratic and anonymous.

Latvia – Reform to Jurisdictions

Reform of Latvia's judicial map was initiated in 2015 and completed by 2018. Prior to the reform, the country had a wide network of courts of first instance, many of which covered small jurisdictions. For example, 65% of district (city) courts were found to have less than 7 judges. In comparison, Riga's city courts heard up to 40% of all civil cases in the country.

In addition, Latvia's judicial system, although three-tiered, was intricately designed with varying levels of jurisdiction assigned to various courts, making the system difficult to understand. The judicial map was transformed to reduce unequal caseload distribution, enhance specialisation of judges, increase the quality of rules, reduce case length and optimise resource allocation. Smaller district courts were combined within the same region, gradually reorganising 34 district courts into 9. In addition to this, one parental court was created in each enlarged district, ensuring the consistent application of laws and provision of services. The level of courts was also revised, removing first instance powers from regional courts. This made the three-tiered system more rational and easier to understand for users.

Finally, reform of the judicial map included the creation of specialised courts. Five courts in particular were established to deal with administrative cases, as well as additional specialised courts for military, tax and land registry matters. These specialised courts are seen as courts of first instance, capable of dealing with sensitive areas of the law.

Source: Della Chiesa, M. (2012), *Comparative Study of the Reforms of the Judicial Maps in Europe*, https://rm.coe.int/comparative-study-of-the-reforms-of-the-judicial-maps-in-europe/168078c53a; Wiertz-Wezenbeck, C. et al. (eds.) (2014), *Judicial Reform in the Netherlands*, www.rechtspraak.nl/SiteCollectionDocuments/judicial-refrom-in-the-Netherlands-2014.pdf; Aavik, M. et al (2018), *Report: Evaluation of the Latvian Judicial System on the Basis of the Methodology and Tools Developed by the CEPEJ*, www.ta.gov.lv/UserFiles/Faili/CEPEJ_Evaluation_Report_Latvia_Final_En.pdf.

Box 2.10. Court specialisation experiences in OECD countries

Norway – Complaint boards and tribunals

Norway uses many different tribunals and complaint boards to supplement the justice system through dispute resolution. Proceedings for these boards are completed in writing, requiring less time than an in-person hearing. They are either free or subject to a modest fee. Some of the boards have incorporated e-justice schemes whereby complaints can be submitted electronically and individuals can follow developments. Since these complaint boards started, a lower number of new civil cases have been brought forward to the courts. These processes have been incorporated into the justice system through the Norway Dispute Act. Norway also uses conciliation boards, which use laypeople instead of members of the judiciary to resolve disputes. These boards are present in almost every municipality as a more approachable forum for justice than the court centre. These boards deal with pecuniary cases and parties to a dispute are obliged to attend before progressing a matter before the court, unless alternative dispute resolution has been attempted in another format.

Canada – Specialised courts

There are 11 specialised courts, including courts for domestic violence, First Nations, integrated courts, drug treatment courts and community courts. Each type has a different objective and approach to therapeutic justice and has been created for a particular issue in the community. The purpose is to deal with underlying reasons for criminal behaviour and to avoid the negative impacts of adversarial courts on defendants, victims and witnesses. The specialised courts are found to have contributed to improving access to health and social service information, efficiency and sentencing options. Partnerships with community organisations have been important in facilitating resources. For example, the Vancouver Downtown Community Court opened in 2008 to deal with city core crime. It is a partnership between 2 levels of court as well as social agencies and deals with 2 000 defendants per year. The domestic violence courts work with community service providers and can hear all domestic violence offences except for the most serious ones. Approximately 50 files are scheduled to be heard on each court date.

Source: Haukeland Fredriksen, H. and M. Strandberg (2016), "Is e-justice reform of Norwegian civil procedure finally happening?", www.idunn.no/oslo_law_review/2016/02/is_e_justice_reform_of_norwegian_civil_procedure_finally_ha; Canadian Ministry of Justice (2016), *Specialized Courts Strategy*, https://www2.gov.bc.ca/assets/gov/law-crime-and-justice/about-bc-justice-system/justice-reform-initiatives/specialized-courts-strategy.pdf.

Management of the judiciary and courts

The measures brought forth by the Justiça + Próxima programme also involve steps to strengthen management of the judiciary and courts, including fiscal and administrative matters, the most significant being the implementation of a case management indicators system in administrative and tax courts.

Portugal has recently introduced a new model of court management, which aims to improve overall efficiency and performance (administrative tasks traditionally belonging to the judge president of each court are now allocated to the court administrator and registrar, thus leaving judges free to exercise their technical legal competencies). This model was introduced with a view of strengthening the quality of management processes in the judiciary. Each district (*comarca*) is headed by a management committee consisting of a president judge (designated by the High Council), a judiciary administrator (designated by the presiding judge among candidates previously selected by the Ministry of Justice) and a representative of the general prosecutor (designated by the High Council of the Public Prosecution). Each party has its own powers and the presiding judge must communicate with the High Council of the Judiciary, the co-ordinating prosecutor with the High Council of the Public Prosecution, and the judiciary administrator with the Ministry of Justice (through the Directorate-General for the Administration of Justice – DGAJ). The administrator, with the general orientation of the presiding judge, can temporarily or permanently relocate court clerks inside the county and under the limits legally established. The presiding judge can propose to the High Council the reallocation of judges or of cases, aiming to even the workload of judges and the efficiency of the court.[19] The co-ordinating prosecutor can reallocate cases and can propose to the High Council of the Public Prosecution the reallocation of public prosecutors.

The committee has the authority to:

- approve the semi-annual and annual reports
- approve a draft budget of the judicial demarcation (*comarca*, based on the pre-determined allocation) to be submitted to the Ministry of Justice
- propose budget modifications
- approve a proposal for the modification of the staff map to be submitted to the Ministry of Justice;
- monitor budget execution.

The measures under the Justiça + Próxima plan (see Annex A for the discussion of roles and responsibilities) also offer the High Council for Administrative and Tax Courts and the Attorney-General Office tools to monitor and evaluate the activity of the courts, contributing to a speedy reaction and within their competencies. The Justiça + Próxima plan also aimed to enable the:

- implementation of an information system to support planning, management and decision-making of district court management bodies
- implementation of an electronic system to manage the distribution and booking of courtrooms.

In 2013, the tax and administrative court territory was divided into four different zones, each presided by a judge. At the court level, the authority lies with the presiding judge of each court of first instance and the judicial administrator (in courts with more than ten judges) or with the secretary of the court (in courts with less than ten judges). At the national level, the management powers for administrative and tax courts of first instance lie with the High Council for the Administrative and Tax Courts. The High Council does not have the competency to set strategic performance goals for courts of first instance but has a number of managerial competencies, in co-operation with the Ministry of Justice, such as setting a caseload and timelines for judges and establishing the criteria for assigning cases to judges.

Experience of OECD and partner countries suggests that judicial efficiency is considered to be affected by other factors such as resources and governance in courts. Improving resource management and good governance within courts can reduce trial length without reducing the quality of judicial decisions (Palumbo et al., 2013). In Portugal, the new court management model has a strong potential to improve overall efficiency and performance. To maximise the impact of the new approach, in line with international evidence (e.g. Palumbo et al., 2013), Portugal may consider options for granting greater autonomy for court presidents, including financial autonomy and budget management matters, in order to support them in achieving the objectives for which they are accountable. For example, court presidents could have greater responsibility for case flow management, including through reporting to the High Council of the Judiciary on very complex cases. Maintaining flexibility, such as the possibility for court presidents to relocate judges to more congested courts, could also help resolve any remaining bottlenecks, also in view of different workloads across the court (Pereira and Wemans, 2017; OECD, 2019).

Importantly, in accordance with growing evidence (e.g. Palumbo et al., 2013), governance of the justice sector matters to ensure the effective functioning of the system. Portugal has recently aligned itself with an increasing international tendency to improve the performance of courts and individual judges through court management mechanisms. In Portugal, Articles 90 and 91 of the Law on the Organisation of the

Judicial System (Law no. 62/2013, of 26 August) mandate the High Judicial Council, the General Prosecutor and the government (Ministry of Justice) to establish procedural objectives for the judicial courts of first instance and prosecutors. Procedural objectives are triennial productivity objectives for each magistrate. Those objectives may be for the whole national territory or specific to each judicial demarcation (*comarca*). The notion of procedural objectives is mainly quantitative (i.e. the number of trials or judicial processes held and their duration) but some case weighting is also mandatory (qualitative notion), as Article 91 determines that, among other factors, the nature, complexity and amount (money at stake) of the cases have to be taken into account while assessing the productivity (i.e. the human and other resources employed in the achievement of the "referential procedural values").[20]

Similarly, management of judicial human resources plays an important role in improving the performance of the judiciary. In Portugal, performance appraisal of judges is done by an inspection body (Judicial Assessment Service), which consists of 20 inspectors who are mainly former judges from the Courts of Appeal, with more than 20 years of experience as judges.[21] The regular performance appraisal of judges is carried out after his/her first year in office and then every four years. The appraisal involves a detailed report with a mark proposal, which has to be ratified by the High Judicial Council, prior to a hearing of the incumbent. The decision of the High Judicial Council may be appealed before the Supreme Court, although, according to the interviewed stakeholders, the appeals appear to be rare.

To strengthen the positive performance impact of the appraisal process and to align the appraisal criteria to the stated objectives of better court management, Portugal may have an opportunity to reflect on the current appraisal processes and indicators with a view to further alignment (e.g. by enhancing attention to quantitative indicators while introducing sound case-weighting mechanisms). In this context, the High Council of the Judiciary approved in 2016 a new regulation for inspections, setting evaluation criteria,[22] which is binding to inspection activities. In particular, the regulation suggests to take into account the following criteria – *inter alia*:

- Productivity (i.e. the resolution rate, which is obtained by dividing the number of processes concluded by the number of processes entered in the same year, and the recovery rate, which is the relationship between closed files and the sum of pending and new files).
- Decision deadlines and procedure lengths, as well as a judge's contribution to annual goals.

Along with these criteria (productivity and speed), Portugal may consider introducing transparent and negotiated case-weighting criteria and a more or less automated distribution of cases, within the limits of the principle of "natural judge".

Administrative and fiscal procedure reform

There are a number of measures included under the Justiça + Próxima plan to modernise administrative and fiscal procedure:

- The One-Stop Shop of the Administrative and Fiscal Courts (*Balcão Único*) started as a pilot project in Sintra and was replicated in all other administrative and fiscal courts from the 1st of January 2018. It allows citizens in any administrative and fiscal court to obtain information and certificates on pending cases, to deliver procedural documents and to consult cases, regardless of the court in which the case is pending.
- The mandatory electronic filing of cases and documents for lawyers and the availability of electronic notifications.
- The extension of SITAF to all superior courts (central administrative courts and the Administrative Supreme Court).

- The above-mentioned implementation of a case management indicators system to administrative and tax courts, offering the High Council for the Administrative and Tax Courts and the Attorney-General Office tools to monitor and evaluate the courts' activity, making for greater efficiency and reactivity within their competencies.

These measures also build on waves of reforms of the administrative and fiscal procedure, most notably in 2001-04,[23] which involved significant innovations in the administrative fiscal judicial organisation by reinforcing some taxpayer guarantees, simplifying the fiscal procedure, amplifying the traditional annulment jurisdiction of administrative and fiscal courts, and giving the judges broader powers. Yet, in accordance with the different stakeholders, due to various constraints (such as limited human resources, namely judges and court clerks, insufficient training, transfer of pending cases to new courts and the malfunctioning of the SITAF information system), the new courts have become congested relatively quickly (Gomes and Fernando, 2017).

In 2015, the jurisdiction of administrative courts was extended to judge on a wider range of cases, for example, on administrative offences related to the violation of urban planning.[24] The administrative procedure was also brought closer to the nature of the civil procedure.

In 2017, the authorities introduced a set of new measures to further rationalise and improve the administrative and fiscal procedure. These included the new[25] and complementary[26] establishment plans for judges for the administrative and fiscal courts, accompanied by a complementary establishment plan, the new establishment plan for administrative and fiscal court inspectors[27] and introduced the One-Stop Shop for Administrative and Fiscal Courts (*Balcão Único*).[28] These were followed by new measures implemented under the Justiça + Próxima programme, such as the extension of the possibility given to parties to consult their judicial cases to all proceedings pending in judicial and administrative and fiscal courts.[29]

In September 2018, the Council of Ministers approved five different legislative actions towards the reform of the administrative and fiscal jurisdiction: i) a draft law to amend the ETAF (the Statute of Administrative and Fiscal Courts), adopting the specialisation of first instance courts, a new management model and a new model for the court support office ;[30] ii) a draft law to amend the procedural regimes of administrative and fiscal cases, aiming at its simplification;[31] iii) a decree-law[32] was approved, foreseeing special measures to reduce the backlog in administrative[33] and fiscal courts; iv) an amendment to the Litigation Costs Regulation was approved,[34] foreseeing a reduction of court costs if the litigant resorts to the use of approved forms (approved but not yet in force)[35] to deliver claims and counterclaims; v) a draft law[36] was approved in order to apply the fiscal enforcement procedure to enforced recovery of court costs.[37]

Alternative dispute resolution

Alternative dispute resolution (ADR) has become a central component of access to justice across OECD member and partner countries. ADR is seen as offering quicker and less expensive solutions, focusing on reconciling parties and offering them the chance of a compromised and sustainable resolution to their dispute and avoiding going to court and related expenses. While there is a growing variety of ADR mechanisms across OECD and partner countries, the most common forms include tribunals, Ombudsman scheme, arbitration, mediation, negotiation, whether court-annexed or not (Box 2.11). ADR mechanisms can also be specialised to meet diverse legal needs, i.e. based on the type of, nature of, or stakeholders to the dispute, e.g. business arbitration, family law mediation, small claims, administrative review, etc. Their binding nature also varies depending on the way they are enforced and incorporated into the country's justice system.

Failing the recourse to or the success of ADR in resolving a dispute, such proceedings continue to allow parties to prepare for a future trial by gathering evidence, for instance. In turn, it can decrease the risks of delay and extra workloads for court personnel and contribute to overall court efficiency by reducing caseloads, limit judicial backlog, streamline trials and cut costs to the justice system.

Box 2.11. Selected ADR approaches in OECD countries

Singapore – Court-annexed ADR

Primary dispute resolution centres were established in Singapore in 1994 as court-annexed ADR services for civil cases. Personal injury or non-injury motor accident claims are automatically referred for ADR, while all other matters are encouraged to attend ADR before trial. A judge can also refer cases to ADR at any time; 7 292 cases were mediated in 2013 and 6 420 in 2014 – at settlement rates of 90% (Menon, 2015). Since 2015, the state has also established the State Courts Centre for Dispute Resolution, which conducts mediations, conciliation and neutral evaluations of cases. Personal injury cases filed in the state courts are managed through this process within eight weeks of filing by the defendant. Claims between CAD 60 000 and CAD 250 000 in district courts are presumed to take part in this process unless they opt out (Singapore State Courts, 2018b).

The Singapore Mediation Centre (SMC) is another mediation provider, which was launched in 1997 by the then Chief Justice as a not-for-profit organisation. It is designed to resolve private commercial matters and works closely with the Supreme Court. The SMC has resolved over 3 600 matters, most of which within one working day. Of the disputants who attended, 84% reported cost savings and 88% reported time savings. More than 94% of attendees said they would recommend the process (Singapore Mediation Centre, 2019). In addition to these methods, Singapore established a Family Justice Court in 2014 as a less confrontational approach to justice. All parents who attend these courts and have children under 21 years of age are required to attend (Singapore State Courts, 2018c).

In order to ensure that ADR is incorporated into the litigation process, the government plays an active role in encouraging litigants through legislation. One of its strengths has been to maintain a pool of experienced mediators, to avoid ADR getting slowed down by a lack of available trained professionals. Two additional mediation schemes have been launched by the Singapore State Courts in 2017. They include an e-negotiation platform for the Community Justice and Tribunals System and a Short Mediation and Hearing initiative. The first allows for secure negotiations to take place in a confidential manner before parties come to court. The second fast tracks cases without complex legal issues (Sundaresh, 2017).

Slovenia – Incentive: Fee Policy

Policymakers have legislated an incentive for parties to reach a settlement through a fee policy. Parties are encouraged to use ADR and a judge can propose a settlement to the parties by way of writing at any stage in the trial. If the parties reach a settlement, two-thirds of the court fee is returned to the claimant, which has amounted to 15%-20% of cases ending in a settlement.

Canada – DRO Program

The Dispute Resolution Officer programme is for parties involved in a child support dispute. Parties must attend a mandatory one-hour session to discuss mediation, attended by a family law specialist who provides neutral advice and works to help the parties resolve a dispute. The programme provides the benefit of a family law practitioner for those who are self-represented and provides parties with some control over the decision. It also streamlines proceedings by requiring necessary forms and basic evidence to be completed prior to appearance.

Sources: Singapore State Courts (2018a), *Overview of Alternative Dispute Resolution*, www.statecourts.gov.sg/cws/Mediation_ADR/Pages/Overview-of-Alternative-Dispute-Resolution.aspx; Menon, S. (2015), "Building sustainable mediation programs: A Singapore perspective", www.americanbar.org/content/dam/aba/publications/dispute_resolution_magazine/fall-2015/10_menon_international_dispatch.pdf; Singapore State Courts (2018b), *Overview of State Courts Centre for Dispute Resolution*, www.statecourts.gov.sg/cws/Mediation_ADR/Pages/Overview-of-State-Courts-Centre-for-Dispute-Resolution.aspx; Singapore Mediation Centre (2019), *Our Achievements*, www.mediation.com.sg/about-us/; Sundaresh, M. (2017), *Advancing Justice: Expanding the Possibilities, Singapore State Courts Annual Report*, https://www.statecourts.gov.sg/cws/Resources/Documents/OJAR_StateCourts_AR_A4_V4.pdf; LUT University (n.d.), "Inventory of caseflow management practices in European civil proceedings: Appendix 1 for the caseflow management handbook", www.lut.fi/documents/27578/419707/Inventory+of+caseflow+management+practices.pdf/51893738-f8fc-4c19-a6d5-28fa5e756347 (accessed 18 February 2019); Government of Alberta (2019), *Dispute Resolution Officer Program*, www.alberta.ca/dispute-resolution-officer-program.aspx.

The Directorate-General for Justice Policy (*Direção-Geral da Política de Justiça*, DGPJ) under the Ministry of Justice oversees the development of all ADR mechanisms (private and public) and support their functioning to some extent.

In Portugal, ADR mechanisms, i.e. Arbitration, Mediation and Justice of the Peace are becoming increasingly popular, and are part and parcel of the latest modernisation efforts:

- *Arbitration* – There are both public and private arbitration centres in Portugal,[38] and – in accordance with the Barometer of Quality of Arbitration Centres – are viewed as beneficial in improving the efficiency of dispute resolution and reducing the backlog of court cases (DGPJ, 2018a). The DGPJ participates in the council of the privately run centres that are responsible for assessing its activities. The DGPJ has consultative powers in these councils, where it gives its opinion about the documents that the centre presents that will then be forwarded to the general assembly. As in many OECD countries, arbitration is specialised in Portugal. For instance, the ministry-supported centres offer services based respectively on consumer, automotive, insurance, industrial property, administrative and tax matters. Most recently the Administrative Arbitration Board, a nationwide private arbitration centre on public procurement, was established.[39] The state and state entities may enter into arbitration agreements provided that the disputes concern private law (as opposed to public law). The Portuguese legislation provides a similar regime for domestic and international arbitration and extends arbitration to other fields such as tax disputes and, in limited cases, labour disputes.
- *Mediation* – Portugal has also established a public and private mediation system[40] (including for family, labour and criminal mediation). Mediation is voluntary and takes place out-of-court. The Ministry of Justice compiles a list of mediators. No specific requirements are needed to register except when the mediator wishes to act within the public mediation systems.[41] The ministry offers non-compulsory certified training. The DGPJ supervises state-run mediators, unlike privately run centres. The only exception goes to the private mediators signed on the list of private mediators managed by the DGPJ. There are 183 public mediators, as well as 566 private mediators signed on the list organised by the Ministry of Justice. The mediation agreement is enforceable directly under specific circumstances if the mediator is registered.[42] The public mediation system is increasingly popular according to Portugal: 30% of family law cases were resolved through public mediation. Yet, while trending positively, public mediation services have the lowest overall satisfaction scoring with 8 out of 10, compared to 8.9 for arbitration and 9.4 for justice of the peace (DGJP, 2018b). Stakeholders also highlighted the importance of providing adequate resources and facilities and enhancing the speed of mediation (DGJP, 2018b). Further efforts to increase the take-up of mediation[43] (DGPJ, 2018b) – possibly through strengthening incentives and communication (e.g. through greater court intervention) and expanding to other areas (e.g. commercial mediation) – would be beneficial in order to reach its full potential. Collecting data from private mediation systems would also allow mapping the extent of the popularity of this mechanism.

- *Justices of the peace* – Twenty-five justices of the peace have jurisdiction for small civil claims (up to EUR 15 000) excluding family, probate and labour matters. They can resort to mediation, conciliation or a simplified court hearing. The decision is appealable in the formal court system if the value exceeds EUR 2 500. Persons may now resort to mediation (except in class actions) and preliminary injunctions are now available.[44] Justices of the peace qualify through a course of conflict mediation recognised by the Ministry of Justice or given by a training entity certified by the DGPJ. The use of the peace courts is subject to a one-time fee of EUR 70 to be borne by the unsuccessful party and the judge may also decide to divide this amount between parties. The use and success of mediation under this mechanism are incentivised under an agreement with the fee of EUR 50, divided between parties.

Such a mix of judicial and out-of-court services is the result of innovative public-public partnership between the justice sector and local authorities (with shared funding). This mechanism for resolving disputes is increasingly popular in Portugal, although remains limited in use (DGPJ, 2018c; UK Law Review, 2018).[45] Between 2001 and 2014, approximately 82 500 claims were heard. There is also scope to strengthen this mechanism by ensuring that there is no overlap with other jurisdictions, greater efficiency (Figure 2.3) and merit-based decision-making (UK Law Review, 2018).[46]

Figure 2.3. Justice of peace cases compared to court cases

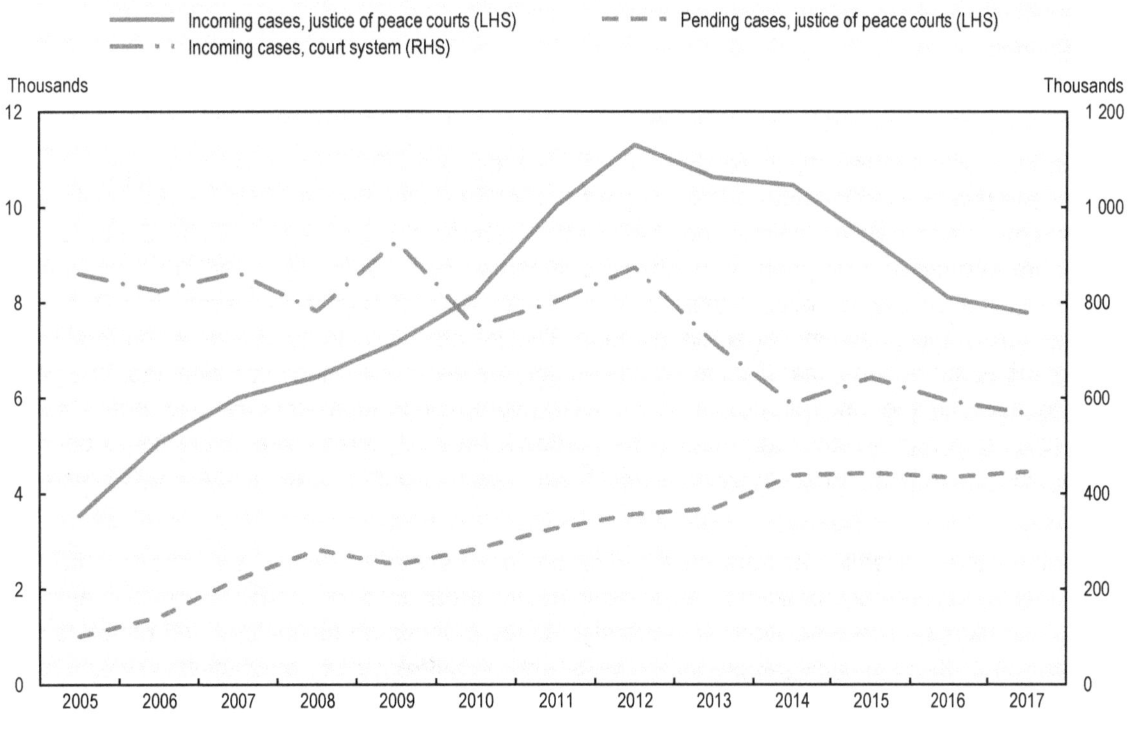

Source: OECD (2019), *OECD Economic Surveys: Portugal 2019*, https://doi.org/10.1787/eco_surveys-prt-2019-en.

Since 2013 the Directorate-General for Justice Policy of Portugal overlooks the Barometers of Quality of Arbitration Centres, the Peace Courts and Public Mediation Systems (with the emphasis on procedural fairness, clarity and timeliness), assessing the satisfaction of their users,[47] and is based on the CEPEJ Handbook for Conducting Satisfaction Surveys. Between 2013 and 2018, user satisfaction has slightly increased and has been stable since 2016, showing continuity in the quality of the public services (Figure 2.4).

Figure 2.4. Public ADR satisfaction increased between 2013 and 2018

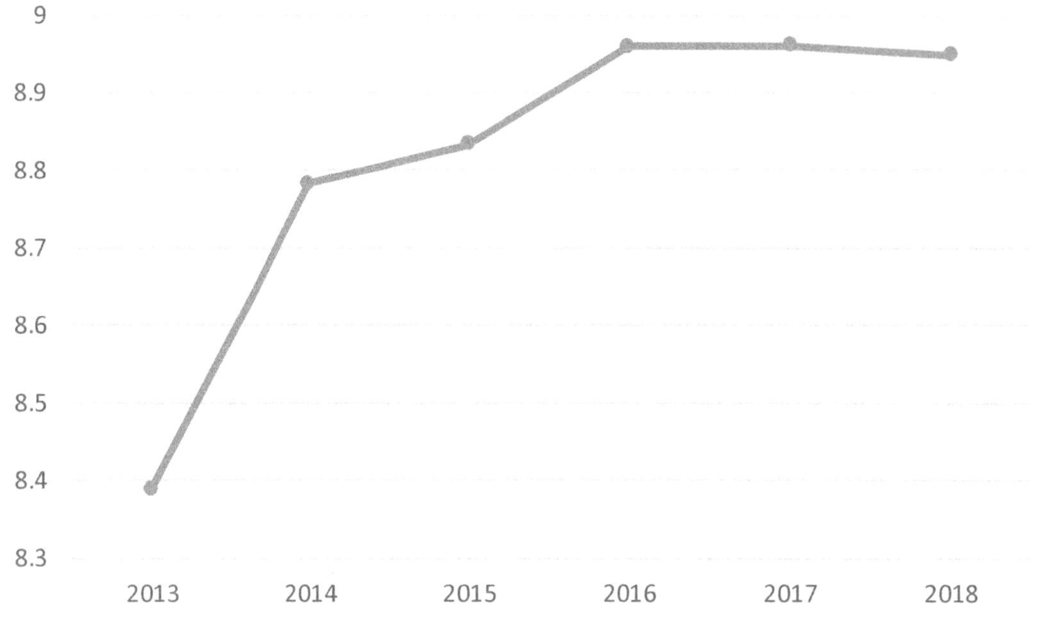

Note: Index: 0-10.
Source: DGPJ (2018a), *Barometers of Quality of Arbitration Centres.*

Developing a people-centred justice service ecosystem that reflects OECD criteria implies the requirement of countries to find ways to integrate ADR along with other resolution processes in a coherent and holistic justice sector vision while maintaining their empowerment (Figure 2.5). When centring service infrastructure and delivery on people's needs, countries can help parties bring their dispute to the right forum. There is a strong potential to facilitate the development of such an ecosystem in Portugal with ADR +, the forthcoming case management platform. This initiative will aim to provide a common stage for justices of the peace in consumer dispute arbitration centres and public mediation systems. The goal is to be interoperable with the new European platform ODR (European Platform for Online Dispute Resolution) and to facilitate access to case information by parties. The next logical step could be to deepen the understanding of the legal needs of citizens, which could help to plan a strategic delivery of ADR across territories.

To strengthen the availability of data on the different mechanisms, it would be important to develop common data management protocols, among others, in order to bridge separate public and private systems for arbitration and mediation. There is also scope to leverage technology and understanding of legal needs in order to ensure geographic accessibility of different ADR mechanisms. In this context, Portugal is continuously looking to adjust and ensure the sustainability of its ADR services network through working groups. In addition, it is developing a new case management platform RaL + (ADR +), which will aim to provide a common platform for justices of the peace in consumer dispute arbitration centres and public mediation systems. This platform will be interoperable with the new European platform ODR (European platform for online dispute resolution). Parties will also have facilitated access to their case information.

Figure 2.5. Integrating ADR in a continuum of legal and justice services

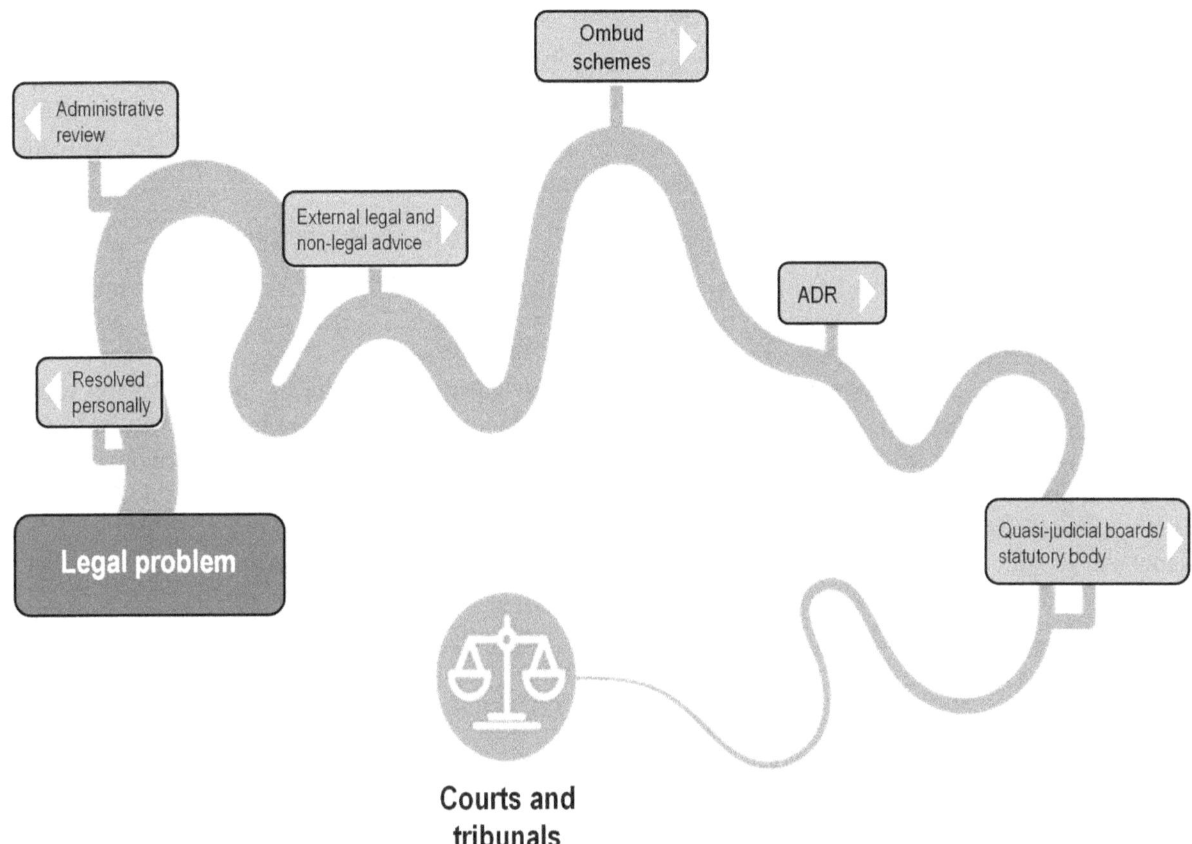

Source: Adapted from Attorney-General's Department of Australia (2009), *A Strategic Framework for Access to Justice in the Federal Civil Justice System, A Guide for Future Action*, Access to Justice Taskforce, https://www.ag.gov.au/LegalSystem/Documents/A%20Strategic%20Framework%20for%20Access%20to%20Justice%20in%20the%20Federal%20Civil%20Justice%20System.pdf.

Innovation for business-friendly justice

To support the improvement of the business climate, Portugal has developed a framework (composed of legislation, innovative technology and procedures) that aims to support Portuguese companies in reinforcing their equity and reducing their levels of indebtedness through various initiatives. For example, in response to the post-crisis rise in insolvency proceedings, Portugal revised the Insolvency Code. In particular, it introduced fast-track approval procedures restructuring plans, such as the Special Revitalisation Process (PER) that seeks to support borrowers in negotiating recovery plans with creditors in case of imminent insolvency. The latter procedure was amended again in 2018, by limiting the availability of the procedure for entrepreneurial activities and viable firms, while creating more simplified special procedures for individuals (OECD, 2019).

Other innovative procedures contemplate extrajudicial procedures such as, for instance, the out-of-court regime for firm restructuring (RERE).[48] These types of extrajudicial procedures have the potential to alleviate the workload within courts and making procedures shorter, more consensual and effective, whilst courts dedicate their resources and time to despatch more complex affairs.

Other initiatives include:

- Out-of-court repossession of the collateral (commercial pledge) legal framework.[49]
- Legal regime for debt to equity swap, including giving the creditors a chance to save companies with or without the equity holders agreement.[50]
- An early warning regime, such as early warning tool of financial self-diagnosis for companies developed by the Agency for Competitiveness and Innovation.[51]
- Electronic proceedings, which are already in force and applicable to insolvency procedures.

While it will take time to see the full impacts of these measures, some of the key results to date include the reduction of pendency in cases linked to businesses as part of the PER process (Figure 2.6). Notably, in accordance with the 2019 OECD Economic Survey, the PER has improved Portugal's firm restructuring regime, as also reflected in World Bank's Doing Business indicators as well as the OECD Insolvency Indicators (Adalet McGowan, Andrews and Millot, 2017). It has contributed to approximately 3 000 cases of firm restructuring over the past 3 years (OECD, 2019). In addition, the 2019 OECD Economic Survey stressed the need for financially attractive alternative dispute resolution schemes for firm liquidation. Such schemes could facilitate co-ordination among creditors, enhance co-operation among parties, help successful liquidation of non-viable firms and reduce costs related to business failure (OECD, 2019).

Figure 2.6. Special revitalisation procedures in the courts of 1st instance, 3rd quarter

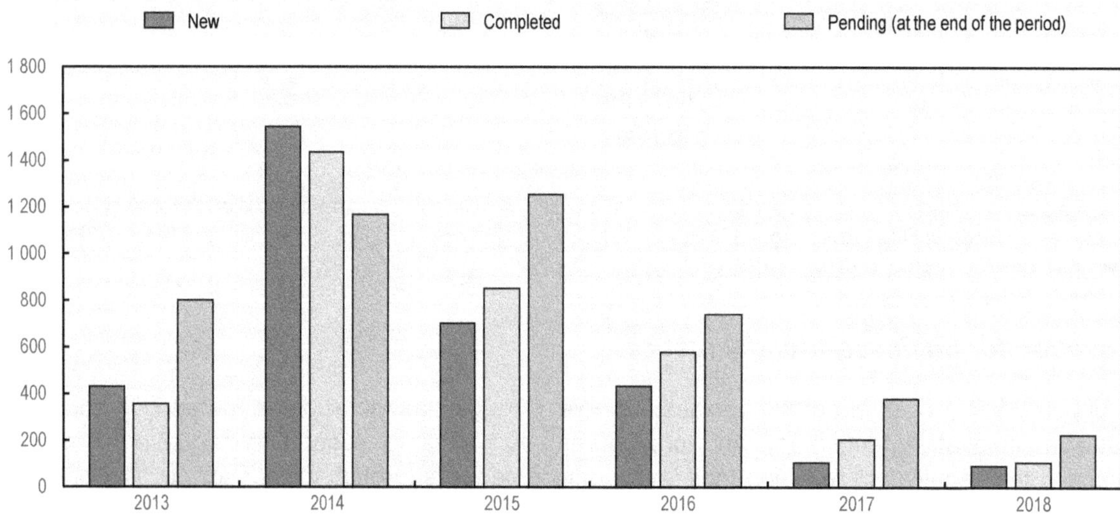

Source: DGPJ (2019), Quarterly Statistical Highlight 60, Quarterly statistics on insolvency cases, on special revitalization procedures and on special procedures for payment agreement (2007-2018).

Enforcement cases

To strengthen enforcement procedures, the Justiça + Próxima programme has integrated a range of measures, including the:

- Development of new features for court clerks to electronically access relevant information on the identification of the debtor and his/her assets.
- Extension of these features to enforcement agents.
- Implementation of a system to identify if an enforcement case is waiting for an act of the court registry or of the judge.

These measures are introduced to reinforce the implementation of reform waves over the past two decades. The first set of reforms was the introduction of enforcement agents in 2002/03.[52] Second is the effort to simplify the enforcement procedure, reduce the intervention of the judge and registrars and enhance the competencies of enforcement agents.[53] It also aimed to promote efficient enforcement procedures, mainly by foreseeing an electronic procedure and allowing enforcement agents to develop a number of activities without judicial consent (such as direct consultation of social security and registry office databases). The third wave was introduced by the new 2013 Civil Procedure Code, which brought five major changes, including:

- *Reducing the range of enforceable titles.* Over the years, procedural reforms have gradually increased the number of enforceable titles, enabling the creditor to start an enforcement procedure without first going through a declarative procedure. The increase of the number of enforceable titles has shifted the courts' backlog from declarative procedures to enforcement procedures, increasing the number of declarative incidents grafted in the enforcement procedure. With the 2013 reform, non-authenticated documents (namely debt confessions and other documents signed by the debtor that acknowledge the existence of a pecuniary obligation) ceased to be considered as enforceable titles and now have to go through a payment order procedure or a civil action.
- *Creating two types of procedures* depending on the type of enforceable title (a faster one, for the more "reliable" enforceable titles, such as court decisions, and another that requires the notification of the debtor prior to the seizure of his/her assets). This modification was intended to guarantee greater certainty and safety in the procedure, introducing stronger control, both by the judge and by the debtor.
- *Moving some of the enforcement agents' competencies to the judiciary.* For example, in ordinary procedures, the court registry is responsible for rejecting the enforcement claim when it does not fulfil the formal requirements. Decisions on the modification of the assets to be seized or on the anticipated sale of seized assets are now under the judge's jurisdiction, for example.
- *Enforcing direct electronic seizure of a debtor's bank accounts* via the enforcement agent or bailiff (rendering a prior judicial decision unnecessary).
- *Limiting the possibility of other creditors being able claim their credits* in a pending enforcement proceeding, thus reducing pending incidents in the enforcement procedure.

Finally, another measure was taken to reduce the backlog in enforcement courts: enforcement cases can also be closed if an enforcement agent does not identify sizeable assets of the debtor within three months. Nonetheless, such proceedings can be renewed whenever the creditor is able to find new assets. The number of pending cases was also reduced as a result of the formal closure of court cases, which were linked to a periodic income. In these cases, enforcement agents award outstanding amounts to the creditors and close the court case, which can also be reopened in case of non-payment.

Notes

[1] Law no. 52/2008 of 28 August (*Lei de Organização e Funcionamento dos Tribunais Judiciais*).

[2] Law no. 41/2013 of 26 June.

[3] Law no. 62/2013 of 26 August.

[4] The Civil Procedure Code has already been amended 6 times: Law no. 122/2015 of 1st September; Law no. 40-A/2016 of 22 December; Law no. 8/2017 of 3 March; Decree-Law no. 68/2017 of 16 June; Law no. 114/2017 of 29 December; Law no. 49/2018 of 14 August.

[5] See Correia and Videira (2016) for a dissenting opinion.

[6] "The principle of the natural judge constitutes a fundamental guarantee of the right to a fair trial. This principle means that no one can be tried other than by an ordinary, pre-established, competent tribunal or judge". See ICJ (2007).

[7] The need to further develop and extend the current system was identified in a study conducted by the DGPJ in 2015. A preliminary draft legislation was developed by the working group and submitted to parliament.

[8] For more information on the Simplex+ programme: https://www.simplex.gov.pt/.

[9] 175 measures approved; 83 concluded; 56 are under development.

[10] The criminal policy goals, priorities and guidelines for the biennium 2017-19 are established under Law no. 96/2017 of 23 August.

[11] For more information see Simplex+ programme: https://www.simplex.gov.pt/.

[12] See also https://ec.europa.eu/info/sites/info/files/justice_scoreboard_2018_en.pdf.

[13] See evaluation of the judicial map at: https://medidasjustica.portugal.gov.pt/avaliacao-do-mapa-judiciario/.

[14] The judicial map was readjusted in January 2017 at https://medidasjustica.portugal.gov.pt/ajustamentos-ao-mapa-judiciario/.

[15] See the list of new videoconferencing and printing equipment for the courts at https://medidasjustica.portugal.gov.pt/novos-equipamentos-de-videoconferencia/ and https://medidasjustica.portugal.gov.pt/novos-equipamentos-de-impressao-para-os-tribunais/.

[16] Law no. 40-A/2016 of 20 December. Tribunal+ also included 44 interventions in court premises (25 completed, 19 ongoing).

[17] See multi-year strategic plan for the redeployment of the courts network at: https://medidasjustica.portugal.gov.pt/plano-estrategico-plurianual-de-requalificacao-e-modernizacao-da-rede-de-tribunais/; www.portugal.gov.pt/pt/gc21/comunicacao/documento?i=plano-estrategico-plurianual-de-requalificacao-e-modernizacao-da-rede-de-tribunais-2018-2028.

[18] See Article 45(1), Law no. 21/85 of 30 July.

[19] Deliberation 756/2018 of the High Council for Judicial Courts regulates on the principles, criteria, requirements and procedure to ensure the reallocation of judges or cases. Any such measures request the consent of the affected judge. The presiding judge must first hear the affected judges and give their consent to the measure. The proposal of application of the measure by the presiding judge to the High Council must indicate the statistical data or other circumstances that justify the measure, the reasons for choosing such measure and the possible alternative measures, the foreseeable duration of the measure,

the goals to be achieved with the measure and the indicators to be used for its final evaluation, and the necessary reorganisation of the services to implement the measure. The High Council has the final ruling.

[20] The law sets limits to the establishment of those procedural objectives for judicial demarcations: they cannot affect in any way judicial decisions on the cases to be adjudicated, neither in matters of substance (merit of the case) nor in terms of the choice of the legally better-suited judicial procedure (procedural fairness).

[21] See the Statute of Judicial Magistrates and the Regulation on the Judicial Inspection of the High Council of the Judiciary.

[22] In accordance with Law no. 62/2013; www.csm.org.pt/wp-content/uploads/2017/02/Novo-Regulamento-dos-Servi%C3%A7os-de-Inspe%C3%A7%C3%A3o-do-Conselho-Superior-da-Magistratura.pdf.

[23] Law no. 15/2001 of 5 June; Administrative and Fiscal Courts Statute (*Estatuto dos Tribunais Administrativos e Fiscais*, ETAF), by Law no. 13/2002 of 19 February; Administrative Procedure Code (*Código de Processo dos Tribunais Administrativos*, CPTA), by Law no. 15/2002 of 22 February.

[24] Decree-law 214-G/2015 of 2 October.

[25] Ordinance no. 2011/2017 of 17 July.

[26] Ordinance no. 288/2017 of 28 September.

[27] Ordinance no. 289/2017 of 28 September.

[28] Ordinance no. 178/2017 of 30 May.

[29] Ordinance no. 267/2018 of 20 September.

[30] Law no. 114/2019 of 12 September.

[31] Law no. 118/2019 of 17 September.

[32] Decree-Law no. 81/2018 of 15 October.

[33] Special teams composed of judges were created to deal with cases pending in administrative and fiscal courts. Also, special incentives (exempting parties from court fees) in withdrawal of cases or in diversion to arbitration were implemented.

[34] Decree-law no. 86/2018 of 29 October.

[35] Ordinance no. 341/2019 of 1 October.

[36] Law no. 27/2019 of 28 March.

[37] See https://www.portugal.gov.pt/pt/gc21/governo/comunicado-de-conselho-de-ministros?i=226.

[38] 35 arbitration centres are authorised by the Ministry of Justice: 10 are supported directly by the ministry and 25 are private.

[39] It was first financially supported by the state. Since 2014 the level of public support has gradually decreased and, in 2017, the centre became privately run.

[40] The 2013 Law on mediation sets out general principles applicable regardless of the entity conducting the mediation (public or private) or the subject matter.

[41] The mediator must hold a mediation certificate issued by an accredited institution or have attended a specific course recognised by the Ministry of Justice/DGPJ. In addition, each public mediation system framework establishes the requirements to become a mediator. These requirements include civil and political capacity, minimum age, professional experience or a university degree, specific training in mediation and fluency in the Portuguese language. Also, the mediator can only integrate the public mediation systems, once s/he is admitted on a public recruitment procedure.

[42] Law no. 29/2013 of 19 April; article 9.º/1 c.

[43] 434 cases being resolved through public mediation in 2017.

[44] As stated in Law no. 78/2001 of 13 July, article 41.º-A, within the limits of the possible material scope of the jurisdiction, whenever someone shows concern that others may cause serious injury or difficulties in claiming of their right, they may apply to the competent justice of the peace court for a preventive or conservatory measure specifically aiming to enforce rights .

[45] Law no. 78/2001 of 13 July (as amended by Law no. 54/2013 of 31 July).

[46] Law no. 78/2001 of 13 July (as amended by Law no. 54/2013 of 31 July).

[47] See report on monitoring of the means of alternative dispute resolution at: https://dgpj.justica.gov.pt/Portals/31/Estudos AIN DGPJ/Relatorio_Satisfacao_Meios_RAL_2018.pdf.

[48] Law no. 8/2018 of 2 March.

[49] Decree-law no. 75/2017 of 26 August.

[50] Law no. 7/2018 of 2 March.

[51] Decree-law no. 47/2019 of 11 April.

[52] Law no. 23/2002 of 21 August, and Decree-law no. 38/2003 of 8 March.

[53] The second one in 2008, with the approval of Law no. 18/2008 of 12 April, and Decree-law no. 226/2008 of 20 November.

References

Aavik, M. et al (2018), *Report: Evaluation of the Latvian Judicial System on the Basis of the Methodology and Tools Developed by the CEPEJ*, CEPEJ, www.ta.gov.lv/UserFiles/Faili/CEPEJ_Evaluation_Report_Latvia_Final_En.pdf.

Acland-Hood, S. (2018), "Modernising the Courts and Tribunals Service", Presentation, HM Courts and Tribunals Service, https://www.ucl.ac.uk/laws/sites/laws/files/ucl_foj_01_03_acland-hood.pdf.

Adalet McGowan, M., D. Andrews and V. Millot (2017), "Insolvency regimes, zombie firms and capital reallocation", *OECD Economics Department Working Papers*, No. 1399, OECD Publishing, Paris, https://doi.org/10.1787/5a16beda-en.

Attorney-General's Department of Australia (2009), *A Strategic Framework for Access to Justice in the Federal Civil Justice System, A Guide for Future Action*, Access to Justice Taskforce, https://www.ag.gov.au/LegalSystem/Documents/A%20Strategic%20Framework%20for%20Access%20to%20Justice%20in%20the%20Federal%20Civil%20Justice%20System.pdf.

British Columbia Legal Services Society (2016), *MyLawBC*, http://factum.mylawbc.com/blog.

Canadian Ministry of Justice (2016), *Specialized Courts Strategy*, Government of British Columbia, https://www2.gov.bc.ca/assets/gov/law-crime-and-justice/about-bc-justice-system/justice-reform-initiatives/specialized-courts-strategy.pdf.

CEPEJ (2018), "European judicial systems – Efficiency and quality of justice", *CEPEJ Studies*, No. 26. European Commission for the Efficiency of Justice, Council of Europe.

CEPEJ (2013), *CEPEJ Revised Guidelines on the Creation of Judicial Maps*, CEPEJ(2013)7Rev1, https://rm.coe.int/1680748151.

Civil Resolution Tribunal (2019), *Welcome to the Civil Resolution Tribunal*, http://civilresolutionbc.ca.

Committee for Justice (2016), "Report on justice in the 21st century: Innovative approaches for the criminal justice system in Northern Ireland", Northern Ireland Assembly, Report NIA 313/11-16, www.niassembly.gov.uk/globalassets/documents/justice-2011-2016/copy-of-the-justice-in-the-21st-century-report-with-appendices.pdf.

Controller and Auditor General (2017), *Ministry of Justice: Modernising Court Services*, New Zealand Government, https://www.oag.govt.nz/2017/courts/docs/courts.pdf.

Correia, P.M.A.R. and Videira, S.A. (2016), "Troika's Portuguese Ministry of Justice Experiment, Part II: Continued positive results for civil enforcement actions in Troika's aftermath", in *International Journal for Court Administration*, Vol. 8(1), pp. 20-31, http://doi.org/10.18352/ijca.215.

Della Chiesa, M. (2012), *Comparative Study of the Reforms of the Judicial Maps in Europe*, Sciences Po Strasbourg Consulting, Strasbourg, https://rm.coe.int/comparative-study-of-the-reforms-of-the-judicial-maps-in-europe/168078c53a.

DGPJ (2019), *Quarterly Statistical Highlight 60, Quarterly statistics on insolvency cases, on special revitalization procedures and on special procedures for payment agreement (2007-2018)*, https://www.dgpj.mj.pt/sections/siej_en/statistical-highlights/annexes/quarterly-statistics-on6002/downloadFile/attachedFile_f0/Dest60__Insolvencies_20190206.pdf?nocache=1549536185.61.

DGPJ (2018a), *Barometers of Quality of Arbitration Centres*.

DGPJ (2018b), *Barometers of Quality of Public Mediation*.

DGPJ (2018c), *Barometers of Quality of Justice of Peace*.

Gomes, C. and P. Fernando (2017), *Justiça e Eficiência - O Caso dos Tribunais Administrativos e Fiscais*, Coimbra, http://opj.ces.uc.pt/site/novo/ficheiros/justica_adm/relatorio_justica_e_eficiencia_taf_23_05_2017.pdf.

Gouveia, M.F., J. Pinto-Ferreira and M. Teixeira (2017), "Evolução do processo civil: Democratização, celeridade e gestão processual", in M. de L. Rodrigues et al. (eds.), *40 Anos de Políticas de Justiça em Portugal*, Almedina, Coimbra, pp. 181-97.

Government of Alberta (2019), *Dispute Resolution Officer Program*, www.alberta.ca/dispute-resolution-officer-program.aspx.

Government of Portugal (2018), *2020 Strategy for Digital Transformation in Public Administration*, https://tic.gov.pt/documents/2018/CTIC_TIC2020_Estrategia_TIC.pdf.

Government of the United Kingdom (2018a), *The HMCTS Reform Programme*, HM Courts and Tribunals Service, https://www.gov.uk/guidance/the-hmcts-reform-programme.

Government of the United Kingdom (2018b), *HMCTS Reform Programme Projects Explained*, HM Courts and Tribunals Service, https://www.gov.uk/guidance/hmcts-reform-programme-projects-explained.

Government of the United Kingdom (2018c), "Quicker way to resolve claim disputes launched online", www.gov.uk/government/news/quicker-way-to-resolve-claim-disputes-launched-online.

Haukeland Fredriksen, H. and M. Strandberg (2016), "Is e-justice reform of Norwegian civil procedure finally happening?", *Oslo Law Review*, Volume 3, www.idunn.no/oslo_law_review/2016/02/is_e-justice_reform_of_norwegian_civil_procedure_finally_ha.

ICJ (2007), *International Principles on the Independence and Accountability of Judges, Lawyers and Prosecutors, Practitioners Guide No. 1,* International Commission of Jurists, https://www.icj.org/wp-content/uploads/2012/04/International-Principles-on-the-Independence-and-Accountability-of-Judges-Lawyers-and-Procecutors-No.1-Practitioners-Guide-2009-Eng.pdf.LUT University (n.d.), "Inventory of caseflow management practices in European civil proceedings: Appendix 1 for the caseflow management handbook", Working Paper, LUT University, www.lut.fi/documents/27578/419707/Inventory+of+caseflow+management+practices.pdf/51893738-f8fc-4c19-a6d5-28fa5e756347 (accessed 18 February 2019).

Ministry of Justice of Portugal (2017), *Court Quality Framework Design Handbook.*

Ministry of Justice of Portugal (2016), *Justiça + Próxima – Plano de Modernizacão e Tecnologia*, Republica Portuguesa.

Ministry of Justice of Portugal (n.d.), *Online Criminal Register*, https://registocriminal.justica.gov.pt.

Morse, A. (2018), "Early progress in transforming courts and tribunals", National Audit Office, https://www.nao.org.uk/press-release/early-progress-in-transforming-courts-and-tribunals/.

My Law BC (2019), *Separation, Divorce and Family Matters*, https://mylawbc.com/.

New Zealand Ministry of Justice (2018a), *Modernising Courts and Tribunals*, New Zealand Government, https://www.justice.govt.nz/about/about-us/our-strategy/modernising-courts-and-tribunals/.

New Zealand Ministry of Justice (2018b), *Statement of Intent*, New Zealand Government, https://www.justice.govt.nz/assets/Documents/Publications/Ministry-of-Justice-statement-of-intent-2017-to-2022.pdf.

OECD (2019), *OECD Economic Surveys: Portugal 2019*, OECD Publishing, Paris, https://doi.org/10.1787/eco_surveys-prt-2019-en.

Otis, K. et al. (2017), *Teleservices: Happening Now!*, Centre for Court Innovation, New York, www.courtinnovation.org/sites/default/files/documents/Teleservices.pdf.

Palumbo, G. et al. (2013), "Judicial Performance and its Determinants: A Cross-Country Perspective", *OECD Economic Policy Papers*, No. 5, OECD Publishing, Paris, https://doi.org/10.1787/5k44x00md5g8-en.

Singapore Mediation Centre (2019), *Our Achievements*, www.mediation.com.sg/about-us/.

Singapore State Courts (2018a), *Overview of Alternative Dispute Resolution*, www.statecourts.gov.sg/cws/Mediation_ADR/Pages/Overview-of-Alternative-Dispute-Resolution.aspx.

Singapore State Courts (2018b), *Overview of State Courts Centre for Dispute Resolution*, www.statecourts.gov.sg/cws/Mediation_ADR/Pages/Overview-of-State-Courts-Centre-for-Dispute-Resolution.aspx.

Singapore State Courts (2018c), *Mediation/Counselling*, https://www.familyjusticecourts.gov.sg/Common/Pages/MediationCounselling.aspx.

Sundaresh, M. (2017), *Advancing Justice: Expanding the Possibilities, Singapore State Courts Annual Report*, Singapore State Courts, Singapore, https://www.statecourts.gov.sg/cws/Resources/Documents/OJAR_StateCourts_AR_A4_V4.pdf.

Taskforce on Justice (2019), *Innovating Justice: Needed and Possible*, Report of the Innovation Working Group of the Task Force on Justice, www.hiil.org/news/innovating-justice-needed-and-possible-report-of-the-innovation-working-group-of-the-task-force-on-justice.

UK Law Review (2018), *The Dispute Resolution Review - Edition 10*, Portugal, https://thelawreviews.co.uk/chapter/1166493/portugal.

Wemans, L. and Pereira M.C (2017), *"Productivity in civil justice in Portugal: A crucial issue in a congested system,"* Economic Bulletin and Financial Stability Report Articles and Banco de Portugal Economic Studies, Banco de Portugal, Economics and Research Department.

Wiertz-Wezenbeck, C. et al. (eds.) (2014), *Judicial Reform in the Netherlands*, Staat der Nederlanden, The Hague, www.rechtspraak.nl/SiteCollectionDocuments/judicial-refrom-in-the-Netherlands-2014.pdf.

3 Court transformation in focus

This chapter explores the role of courts in the justice system transformation. It presents the scope, measures and principles, functioning and delivery models of the Tribunal + programme in Portugal.

Courts as frontliners for justice system transformation

A modern and people-centred justice ecosystem encompasses a growing spectrum of integrated and interlinked formal and non-judicial services. Ensuring equal access to justice means providing the right mix of legal and justice services, which varies from country to country and evolves based on the necessities to respond to legal needs. In all countries, judiciaries and courts are key players and service providers in this ecosystem and, as such, co-leaders in justice service transformation.

Until recently court performance focused on supply aspects that are easily quantifiable, namely those related to efficiency or productivity e.g. collected by internal case management system such as disposition rate (OECD, forthcoming). With the nature of the courts and other justice institutions changing to be more service-oriented and to deliver better justice services for all, judiciaries and courts are today exploring innovative approaches to adopting people-centred perspectives that are responsive to their legal needs and sustain their resolution. These demand-driven initiatives have impacts on their governance structure, monitoring frameworks (including legal needs survey) and better targeting resources to specific needs in the context of fiscal constraints.

Yet identifying indicators that reflect the impact of a justice intervention on how people's legal problems are resolved remains a global challenge (OECD, 2019). The OECD criteria are a starting point for a process of continual learning and evolution of evidence-based best practice to ensure high-quality judicial (and broader justice) service planning and delivery (OECD, 2019).

The Portuguese justice system is taking active steps towards user-centred orientation. More specifically, as part of the Tribunal + project, pilot courts are driving transformation and changing the nature of their operations, leveraging on technology and rationalisation at the front and back ends, with impacts on judges, prosecutors, clerks, lawyers, users and other stakeholders.

What is Tribunal +?

As part of the Justiça + Próxima programme, the Tribunal + project was designed to address the following gaps in the Portuguese justice system:

- High procedural pendency, causing direct and indirect costs to citizens and economic agents and negatively affecting the image of justice.
- Perception of the existence of human resources insufficient to cover needs.
- The need to simplify and improve efficiency, in particular in tasks inherent to the front offices and court registry.
- The large volume of paper in the procedural flow, making dematerialisation a priority.
- The need to adapt the form of relationship to different users (e.g. citizens, companies, agents) and their needs.

Tribunal + was designed on the basis of a needs assessment carried out in April 2016 and tested as a pilot project in the Court of Sintra in September 2016, with the ability and opportunity to iterate and improve. The rollout of the project is planned in phases, in order to develop manageable and enforceable steps, whilst continuing to benefit from direct and continual input from service users.

The project was implemented in the other courts of West Lisbon County in 2017 and is currently being extended to the rest of the country (Figure 3.1).

Figure 3.1. Tribunal + rollout milestones

Source: Provided by the Ministry of Justice of Portugal, 2019.

The project introduced changes to the court's operation in the following three areas (Figure 3.2 and Table 3.1):

- Front office: a new attendance model (Balcão +) for receiving citizens in court and responding to their legal needs – including, when necessary, a face-to-face meeting with a prosecutor.
- Back office: the re-engineering of work processes for clerks and a new organisation based on team management and daily monitoring of workflows, and greater specialisation of clerks.[1]
- Technology: the introduction of new information technology (IT) equipment and solutions, including the automation of notifications and outsourcing of delivery to individuals ("printing and finishing"), the digitalisation of all documents and dematerialisation of the process for opening a case in civil matters, additional computers and display screens providing information on the day's trials in every court (as discussed above).

Figure 3.2. What is Tribunal +

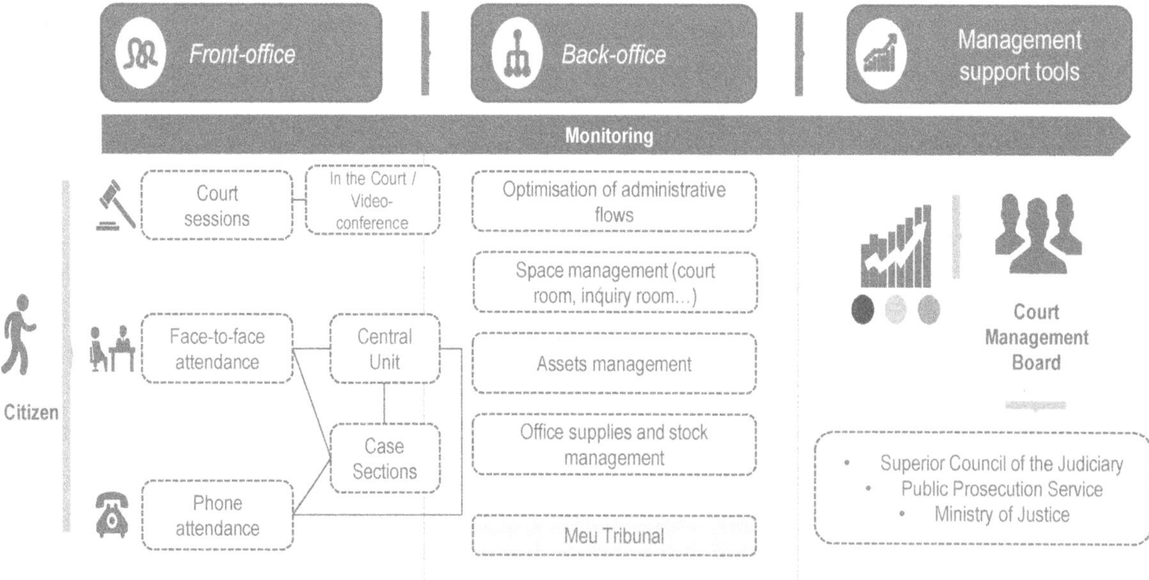

Source: Provided by the Ministry of Justice of Portugal, 2019.

Figure 3.3. Elements of Tribunal +

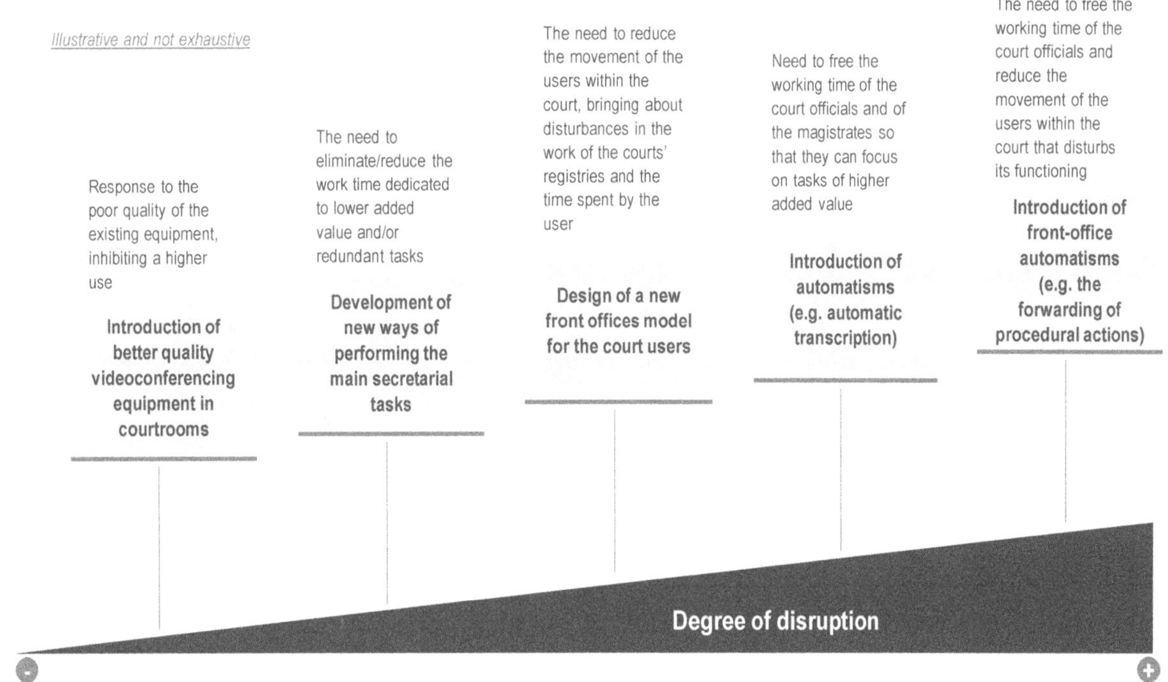

Source: Provided by the Ministry of Justice of Portugal, 2019.

Table 3.1. Tribunal + measures and general principles

Front office	Back office	Technological solutions
More efficient assistance	Administrative and procedural simplification	Digitalisation of documents and development of user-friendly platforms
Screen citizens during 1st contact Minimise the need for citizens to walk inside the building Promote alternative channels to in-person visits to the court (i.e. less need to go to the court if the citizen can solve his/her issues remotely and/or in another place/entity)	Scope -analysis: • Flows • Volumes • Teams Implementation of a process management indicators system allowing the Attorney General's Office and Superior Council (within their competencies) to monitor and evaluate the activity of courts, with updated data, for efficient performance Implementation of an information system to support planning, management and decision-making, for optimisation of human, material and financial resources	*Non-exhaustive* Automatic transcription at the judicial level • Hearing of witnesses who are in another district and detained • Hearing experts' statement for future reference • Minimise repetition of traumatic events by victims • Alerts and notifications by SMS and emails • "Meu Tribunal" system solution to monitor and report intervention needs • Access to Citius web portal by judicial administrators • Electronic consultation of cases by citizens
Balcão + (centralised assistance) • General support: criminal record, requirements, documents, certificates, payments • Specialised assistance: Department for Investigation and Penal Action, Civil/Commerce/Enforcements Civil Law/ Labour • Assistance to citizens with reduced mobility/	Training in assistance Training for relevant support actions Training in technological solutions, applications and equipment	At management level • Meetings of the management bodies • Share of information • Automatic transcription • Swift registration and review • More user-friendly search • PEPEX system for list of public debtors • Electronic communication by National

Front office	Back office	Technological solutions
More efficient assistance	Administrative and procedural simplification	Digitalisation of documents and development of user-friendly platforms
assisted support/self-service Decentralised consideration of cases • Family and minors • Criminal • Administrative and fiscal		Industrial Property Institute and Intellectual Property Court • Electronic communication between registries and courts in relation to parental regulation • Expanding Citius to criminal procedures in view of promotion/protection of family and minors' procedures • Justice fees simulator • Electronic communication between courts and other public entities, such as social security and health ministry • Going digital – Digital proximity

Source: Based on the information provided by the Ministry of Justice of Portugal.

Court front office and attendance model (Balcão +)

As suggested in the Tribunal + project, a single point of entry ensures that court users are greeted and provided with assistance from the moment they walk into the court centre. As court users may be attending for a variety of reasons, including legal advice, court hearings, filings, ticket payments or general queries, having a system to triage these questions and provide timely answers is essential. Effectively triaging court users can resolve simple questions easily and prevent court users from walking further into the centre unnecessarily and can be assisted by signage, staff and welcoming procedures to guide users further. In addition to a physical first point of entry, court users may come into contact with the court centre via the Internet or by telephone. In line with good international practices (see Box 3.1), Tribunal + is increasingly putting in place a system to channel concerns and guide users to a resolution in order to save time and costs. It will also aim to put a phone directory in place, publish information on the court website and use social media to disseminate updates in order to facilitate a user-friendly court experience.

Box 3.1. Selected examples of court front-office modernisation efforts in OECD countries

United States – Wayfinding and signage

In Californian courts, wayfinding design strategies have been found to compensate for a lack of signage. Functions such as public service counters, information and self-help are located at the main entrances as they attract a high volume of court users. This information should be easy to locate and access without an individual needing to walk into and through the court centre. Throughout the building, signage should be located in high-traffic areas for self-represented litigants and translated into multiple languages if necessary. Iconography is also used for standard notices such as offices, services and regulations.

Best practice courts displayed a calendar of the docket in lobby areas as well as outside courtrooms. They also utilised an electronic queuing system in the form of a freestanding kiosk, where users can select a reason for their visit and wait in a comfortable sitting area until their number is displayed. Using a system such as this reduces long waiting lines and allows the centre to better allocate staff resources. Electronic systems also provide multi-language options for increased accessibility. It is recommended to involve court staff in the design and implementation of signage as they can advise on usability and functionality in order to develop a user-responsive approach. It is also important to conduct assessments of signage and welcoming procedures with staff and local groups interacting with court users on a regular basis.

Canada – Seamless access to justice in French language pilot project

Launched in Ottawa in 2015, the pilot was an 18-month project run by the Ministry of the Attorney General and Ontario's Chief Justices. "This is the first time a collaborative effort has been made in a specific location to enhance access to justice in French and to address potential challenges faced by francophones seeking to access services in French or to exercise their language rights under the Courts of Justice Act or the Criminal Code of Canada". The primary objectives were to provide co-ordinated access to services in French, promote awareness of French-language rights, reduce challenges for these litigants, identify best practices, use technology to enhance French services and encourage other partners to participate. The pilot offered:

- Counter ticketing system – Q-Matic system that is bilingual and allows clients to choose a ticket in English or French, alerting staff when a user has taken a French-language ticket.
- Public-facing screens with English and French messages.
- Bilingual court list templates.
- Bilingual greetings to the public to initiate communication.
- Phonetic spelling to enable English-speaking staff to assist, monitored by phone and counter audits.
- Entry in an electronic database detailing whether a case is in French or English.
- French grammar software, lessons for bilingual staff and interactive training sessions.

It is necessary to consider all aspects of communication when providing multilingual access to justice; this includes counter service, telephone directories, emergency announcements and courtroom announcements. Visual aids such as signage, forms, stickers, screens and badges can all be used to guide court users or indicate multilingual assistance.

Source: Language Access Plan Implementation Task Force (2017), *Wayfinding and Signage Strategies for Language access in the California Courts: Reports and Recommendations*, www.courts.ca.gov/documents/LAP-Wayfinding-and-Signage-Strategies-Language-Access-in-the-CA-Courts.pdf; Ministry of the Attorney General (2017), *Seamless Access to Justice in French Pilot Project*, www.attorneygeneral.jus.gov.on.ca/english/about/pubs/access_to_justice_in_french/.

After initial entry, finding directions and signage are essential to guide users to the appropriate location in a timely manner. As also found in the Sintra project, docket information upon entry and outside each courtroom, floor information inside lifts or stairwells, maps and safety information, and easily-identifiable words as well as icons can be effective in facilitating access. To further strengthen the Tribunal + initiative offering, it could be useful to introduce multi-use spaces and flexible rooms for users to hold breakout sessions or resolution discussions in private (Department of Justice, 2017). Other services a court might consider are childcare facilities and service dogs, both of which can provide necessary assistance for vulnerable members of the public and lead to a more therapeutic environment whether they are seeking assistance or attending a hearing (Department of Justice, 2017).

As part of the Tribunal + project, a prototype of a court's front desk was developed through a series of workshops attended by clerks by mapping business processes, with ergonomics and better citizen service in mind (Figure 3.4). As of mid-March 2019, 48 courts integrated the new attendance model and issued around 220 000 attendance tickets and over 27 000 automatic presence declarations.

Court back office

There is an increase in the use of new technologies to improve the performance of justice systems and make more efficient the services they provide to users (Box 3.2). The Tribunal + project also focuses on identifying efficiencies in back office processes and promoting automation of certain tasks, as developed below in the description of the Sintra pilot project. By shortening the time needed to file a case or to provide relevant documents for a decision, the project is expected to impact the workload of judges indirectly. Also, by releasing court clerks from unnecessary tasks, it will make it possible to allocate resources to more qualified tasks, provided that there is adequate training for those more demanding tasks. Currently, daily work organisation methodology implemented in 23 process units and 20 court clusters (comarcas) employ the new office set up approach in 74 buildings.

Figure 3.4. Attendance model in Tribunal +

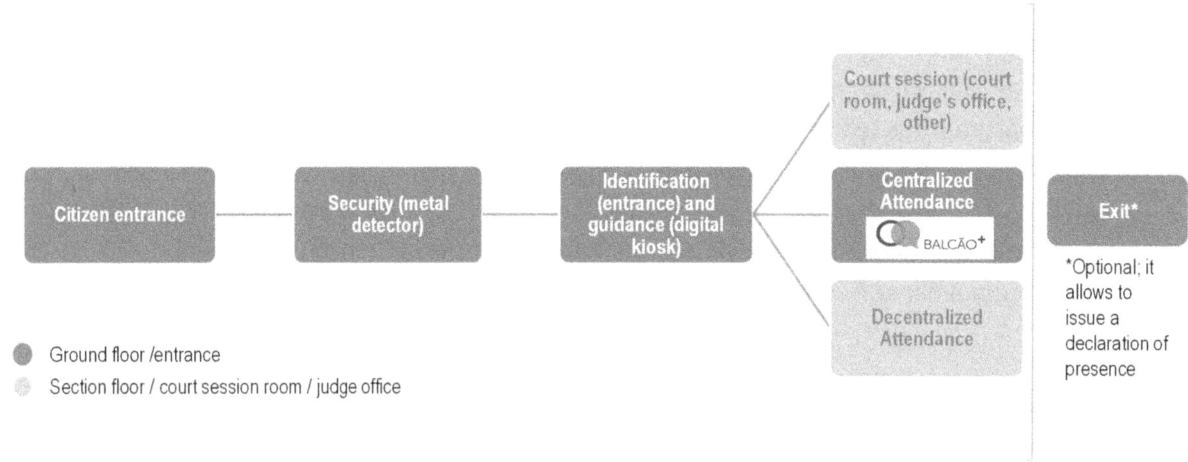

Source: Provided by the Ministry of Justice of Portugal, 2019.

The Portuguese authorities recognised that new work methodologies and a new attendance model bring new challenges and additional training needs. To this end, training in attendance was developed and included:

- *Training in judicial techniques*. The training was designed to be delivered both in a classroom and on the job, in order to address the new methods to be used in assistance and welcome desk (Balcão +) and in the court registrar. It is intended to be provided by the General Directorate of Justice Administration (DGAJ) in close partnership with the consultant on change management. In order to spread knowledge provided by such training activities, training will be applied to the key elements of the rollout courts by court clerks ("ambassadors") who have partaken in previous pilot projects (cascade model).
- *Technical training in solutions/technological applications and equipment*, such as the front-office kiosk, attendance management solutions and videoconferencing. These training activities will be provided by the suppliers of each of the technological solutions.

Box 3.2. Technology for court efficiency

Austria – Justice 3.0

Austria has led a series of justice innovations with information and communication technology (ICT). Phase 1 saw data processing innovations take place between 1980 and 2000, while Phase 2 implemented Internet technology, networking and service-oriented IT procedures between 2000 and 2015. Phase 3, or the Justice 3.0 project, is now underway and is moving towards complete digitisation of processes, high-quality user-experience applications and cognitive technologies. The pilot programme was launched in 2016 and upgrades and training measures are expected to be implemented in all judicial offices by 2020. Common principles of the project are to use modern technology to create:

- concurrent access to a digital file
- remote mobile access
- flexible allocation of tasks
- choice between paper and digital work
- possibilities for autonomous work
- automated proceedings
- joint management of parties' participation in the process
- task management with process patterns
- primarily electronic communication within the justice system
- primarily electronic delivery of documents
- full information on fees
- search and process functions for all file contents
- automated appointments and calendars.

The project will integrate all existing IT modules to deal with legal proceedings and file management and create a digital file. Judges will be equipped with multi-touch tablets as well as touchscreen monitors and a signature pad to allow for navigation of the system as well as studying files. PDF file creation will be possible as well as electronic delivery of paper documents, preventing file delays waiting for the receipt of documents.

An automated task list will also be created for each unit, to visualise appointments for case files that are in progress. This system will incorporate incoming mail from the clerk, accounts manager, cost auditor, assistant, and judge into an electronic file or create a new entry if a file does not yet exist. This will enable offices to work in a more comfortable manner, reduce the need to transport files between offices and allow for audits at any given time. Anticipated benefits of the programme are to reduce proceedings by 20% as well as generate savings of EUR 30 million in personnel costs, EUR 50 million in material costs and EUR 150 million for citizens and the economy. In total, the government forecasted total savings for the judiciary of EUR 230 million per year. In 2017, 14.7 million transactions were completed under the pilot, including 4.8 million e-filings and 7.6 million electronic deliveries. The cost per electronic delivery was EUR 0.07, amounting to savings on postage fees of EUR 12 million (Schneider, 2018). The project was awarded a Best Practice Certificate in 2015 by the European Public Service Awards (EIPA, 2015).

Canada – Court Administrative Technology Suite

British Columbia launched an e-court programme called the Court Administrative Technology Suite, as a joint initiative between the Ministry of Attorney General, the Court Services Brand and all three levels of the British Columbian judiciary. The project was launched to create an integrated system for the seamless co-ordination of electronic documents from law offices to registries, judicial desktops and the courtroom. It was designed to include electronic courtrooms, a complete electronic case file, an integrated system for real-time monitoring in the registry, electronic exhibit management and links to information systems. The goal was to support public access, remote access by court personnel and in-court functionalities.

The project was completed in incremental stages over a period of 15 years and showcases why a well-explained vision can enable widespread adoption and general success of the imitative. At first, two modules were designed and became the basis of the project. This included case management systems for criminal matters as well as civil, family and estate cases. Development of these systems evolved from case tracking to case management, an essential component of the e-search application launched at a later date. The initial focus for in-court functionality relied on consultative discussions before directions were issued to the public. Additions to facilitate in-court technology were later rolled out, including evidence presentation cards and revisions to court staff roles. Paper forms were then eliminated and electronic proceedings were made possible. Project discussions included a wide variety of stakeholders, in particular the judiciary, which was key in the planning, implementation and acceptance of the system. This also led to a better understanding of the diversity of court users and the relationship between court systems and workflow.

In 2011, the first electronic case proceeding took place at the Supreme Court and in 2012, the first electronic proceeding before the Court of Appeal. During the appeal, a working group made up of judges, court services branch employees, senior policy analysts, and technology and business consultants was established. Each of the five judges on the panel had been involved throughout the planning stage of the project and their workspaces were already organised to suit their technological needs and preferences.

The Netherlands – Quality and Innovation

The Netherlands sought to modernise its civil and administrative procedure through its Quality and Innovation project announced in 2012. The Ministry of Security and Justice and the High Council of the Judiciary were in close co-operation throughout the project. Prior to reform, the system was heavily paper-based and the project sought to include more standard, user-friendly digital procedures. Case management software was developed called MyCase, allowing for the uploading of initial documents and the creation of a court staff workspace. Discussions took place step by step between future users, modifying the programme as needed. This was linked with legislative reform, involving discussions with judges, court personnel and lawyers. The software will immediately react to litigation events, responding to court calendars and decreasing the amount of time a file takes to complete. The project is estimated to create a cost reduction of EUR 270 million annually.

Sources: Hackl, M. (2018), "e-Justice in Austria from CDO perspective", www.venjitour.nl/sites/default/files/presentation%20e-justice%20in%20Austria%202018_CDO_v4.2_compressed_pub.pdf; Gesek, C. (2016), "Justiz 3.0", www.justiz.gv.at/web2013/home/e-justice/justiz-30~2c94848b5461ff6e01562be726d72d43.de.html; Schneider, M. (2018), "e-Justice in Austria from CIO perspective", https://www.venjitour.nl/sites/default/files/presentation%20e-Justice%20in%20Austria%202018_CIO_v4.1_compressed.pdf; EIPA (2015), *List of EPSA 2015 Best Practice Certificate Recipients: European, National and Regional Level*, http://www.epsa2015.eu/files/EPSA2015_Best_Practices_EU_Nat_Reg.pdf; Lupo, G. and J. Bailey (2014), "Designing and implementing e-justice systems: Some lessons learned from EU and Canadian examples", www.mdpi.com/2075-471X/3/2/353; De Weers, T. (2016), "Case flow management net-project – The practical value for civil justice in the Netherlands", https://www.iacajournal.org/issue/21/file/50/.

Pilot project: Sintra

In order to test the effectiveness of the Tribunal + model, the Portuguese government has designed a series of pilot projects, first and foremost in the Court of Sintra. The pilot projects aim to assess costs and benefits and identify lessons learned before a national rollout. The Sintra pilot offers the public a new front office model, the simplification of information flows in the back office (court secretariats) and the introduction of management support and productivity tools.

The pilot aims to transform the court operations by changing the complex processes and labour-intensive, paper-based systems which were seen as creating errors, duplication and inefficiency. It is based on a three-level intervention, in line with the logic of Tribunal +. First, it aims to improve user experience, by: providing for a new customer service model – Balcão +; creating new functionalities (such as the possibility of automatically issuing an attendance slip at the front-office kiosk); developing automated tasks; improving assistance and waiting areas; promoting intuitive communication and a new image. Second, it aims to improve secretarial tasks, by speeding registry procedures based on the evaluation provided by the Kaizen Institute and promoting the automation of certain tasks, such as automatic transcription or online criminal record requests. Third, it looks to introduce tools to support court management, such as court hearing management software, asset management software, energy efficiency monitoring software, office supplies management software and a system for evaluating public and internal satisfaction. The change is underpinned by greater use of technology – including video-enabled hearings, improved scheduling and listing, more wi-fi and screens, and automatisation, including of the front office.

The logic behind the proposed design of the Tribunal + project is that the new attendance model is expected to modify the distribution of user demands between the four existing types of attendance – centralised, decentralised and remote (telephone, online) attendance, as well as court sessions, to increase the effectiveness and efficiency of frontline services for each of these types of attendance, and to generate implementation costs (investment in equipment, training, reorganisation of services). These outcomes are expected to increase user satisfaction, reduce the average time spent by users to complete a procedure – at least in the case of simple procedures – and modify the level of human resource required in front-office services for each type of attendance. The latter outcome is expected to lead to a reduction in front-office backlog and to open up the possibility of reallocating resources between services/types of attendance, which in turn – together with the effects of back-office reforms – would lead to better case flows, higher clearance rates and shorter proceedings, as well as increased specialisation of judges and courts. Finally, the various aspects of improved court performance would trigger positive socioeconomic outcomes such as enhancing the rule of law, increasing hours of work (by lowering absenteeism), etc. (see below).

Box 3.3. Streamlining court operations

The Sintra pilot project Tribunal + has benefitted from analysis on attendance and phone call flows, on the productivity of court clerks, the activities of registries, lead time of closed cases and on the dimension and dynamics of each court clerk team. Based on such assessment, the following actions have been recommended:

1. Centralise face-to-face and phone attendance. Each unit (that can comprise multiple judges) shall have a single point of attendance, guaranteed by a single court clerk assigned in turn on a weekly or daily basis.
2. Simplify six essential tasks of the registry: joining documents, notifications, accounting procedures, internal transportation of judicial proceedings, regular post receipt and archive

management. Solutions were presented either to change the ergonomics of the workplace, to resort to automation innovations or to reduce redundant activities.

It has also been recommended to implement daily improvement routines to each registry, by ensuring the organisation of the physical and digital workplace and by promoting regular team meetings to evaluate ongoing progress and assess the completion of target goals. Each registry's internal assessment is carried out via a physical dashboard that is continuously updated to keep track of teams' daily achievements, stimulating competition between them.

Source: Provided by the Ministry of Justice of Portugal, 2019.

Rollout of the Tribunal + project

Tribunal + was extended to three other courts of the West Lisbon district in January 2017, started being implemented in the rest of the country in October 2017 and is expected to be completed in 2019 (Figure 3.5). The implementation schedule and conditions have been adapted to the specific requirements of each of the three components. The rollout of back-office measures, in particular, is placed under the responsibility of the district cluster management committees, with the technical assistance and under the supervision of the ministry. Emphasis is placed on selecting and training trainers within the clerical staff of each court cluster, thereby making them the agents of future change.

In particular, the Attendance + (Balcão +) model was extended to the West Lisbon district (Amadora, Cascais and Sintra). Each court experimented with the specialised services, including:

- Sintra – Civil/commercial/enforcement/labour cases.
- Cascais – Civil and labour cases.
- Oeiras – Civil and enforcement cases.
- Amadora – Family, minors and civil cases.

Figure 3.5. Chronogram of the Tribunal + Project

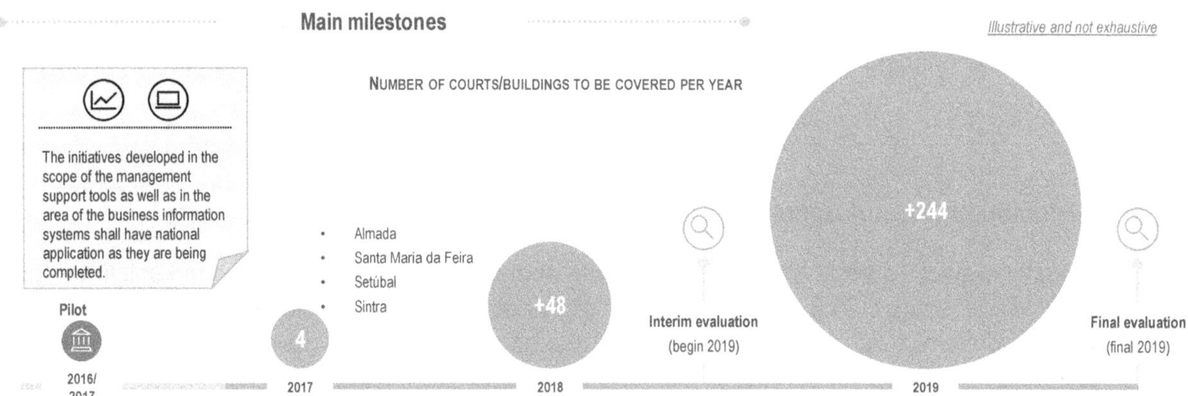

Source: Provided by the Ministry of Justice of Portugal, 2019.

The rollout was accompanied by a series of workshops to facilitate the implementation of the model, as well as efforts to simplify processes to deal with incoming and outgoing correspondence. Each pilot court will follow the implementation in courts from different clusters according to their size. Initial training will be provided to judicial administrators, clerks at the top of the hierarchy and personnel from the DGAJ who will help with the implementation.

Looking ahead, it would be important to put in place an effective monitoring and evaluation framework, as well as a robust approach to sound scaling up of the project to ensure its sustainability and impact (see Chapter 4).

Notes

[1] An external consultancy has been hired to conduct the re-engineering of clerical work, following a template from the manufacturing industry. Workshops have been organised with clerks from every department of the court. Each workshop has mapped and broken down the workflows into individual tasks, analysed the time used on and the value-added of each task, and rationalised the workflow on this basis.

References

De Weers, T. (2016), "Case flow management net-project – The practical value for civil justice in the Netherlands", *International Journal for Court Administration*, Volume 8(1), https://www.iacajournal.org/issue/21/file/50/.

Department of Justice (2017), *Design Brief for Courthouses in Western Australia*, Government of Western Australia, Perth, https://courts.justice.wa.gov.au/_files/courts_design_brief.pdf.

EIPA (2015), *List of EPSA 2015 Best Practice Certificate Recipients: European, National and Regional Level*, http://www.epsa2015.eu/files/EPSA2015_Best_Practices_EU_Nat_Reg.pdf.

Gesek, C. (2016), "Justiz 3.0", Long video transcript, Austrian Federal Ministry of Justice, www.justiz.gv.at/web2013/home/e-justice/justiz-30~2c94848b5461ff6e01562be726d72d43.de.html.

Hackl, M. (2018), "e-Justice in Austria from CDO perspective", Presentation, Austrian Federal Ministry of Constitutional Affairs, Reforms, Deregulation and Justice, The Hague, www.venjitour.nl/sites/default/files/presentation%20e-justice%20in%20Austria%202018_CDO_v4.2_compressed_pub.pdf.

Language Access Plan Implementation Task Force (2017), *Wayfinding and Signage Strategies for Language access in the California Courts: Reports and Recommendations*, Judicial Council of California, San Francisco, www.courts.ca.gov/documents/LAP-Wayfinding-and-Signage-Strategies-Language-Access-in-the-CA-Courts.pdf.

Lupo, G. and J. Bailey (2014), "Designing and implementing e-justice systems: Some lessons learned from EU and Canadian examples", *Laws*, Vol. 2014/ 3, pp. 353-387, www.mdpi.com/2075-471X/3/2/353.

Ministry of the Attorney General (2017), *Seamless Access to Justice in French Pilot Project*, www.attorneygeneral.jus.gov.on.ca/english/about/pubs/access_to_justice_in_french/.

OECD (2019), *Equal Access to Justice for Inclusive Growth: Putting People at the Centre*, OECD Publishing, Paris, https://doi.org/10.1787/597f5b7f-en.

OECD (forthcoming), *Strengthening Local Legal Institutions for Inclusive Growth and Sound Investment Climate in Mexico - Policy Highlights*.

Schneider, M. (2018), "e-Justice in Austria from CIO perspective", Presentation, Austrian Federal Ministry of Constitutional Affairs, Reform, Deregulation and Justice, The Hague, https://www.venjitour.nl/sites/default/files/presentation%20e-Justice%20in%20Austria%202018_CIO_v4.1_compressed.pdf.

4 Sustaining a transformed people-centred justice sector

This chapter examines approaches to enhance the sustainability of the current justice reform agenda in Portugal. It puts a particular emphasis on evaluation and monitoring, including measurement of the justice sector performance, indicators, cost-benefit analysis and stakeholder assessments. It aims to provide for a robust analytical framework based on a detailed theory of change and enhanced data collection processes.

Evaluating and monitoring progress

Measuring the performance of the justice sector

In consultation with the High Council of the Judiciary and the office of the General Prosecutor, the Ministry of Justice has developed a set of strategic performance goals and key performance indicators. The performance assessment framework applies to all courts of first instance and public prosecution offices at the court, process and individual judge/prosecutor levels. The indicators, which are intended to measure the efficiency, effectiveness and quality of the courts, consist of:

- The clearance rate.[1]
- The disposition time.[2]
- Pending cases awaiting final decision.
- Pending cases after final decision.
- Percentage of pending cases with duration above the reference value.
- Average duration of pending cases.
- Average duration of completed cases.

Court performance is monitored on this basis at the local level and nationally, through quarterly meetings between representatives of the High Council of the Judiciary, the High Council of the Public Prosecution and the Ministry of Justice. This allows both the management of district clusters and the High Council to monitor performances and workloads and allocate resources accordingly.

Successive judicial reforms have increased the reliability and granularity of court-level data in Portugal but they have also introduced some discontinuities in the data that make the analysis of recent trends more challenging.[3] Further changes are currently being introduced.[4] Continuing efforts to strengthen the reliability of the data and to better exploit disaggregated data (based, for example, on the quality and complexity of cases and the cost of litigation) would support a more in-depth assessment of court performance (OECD, 2019).

More fundamentally, the international practice points towards the importance of extending the analysis to other aspects of court performance and other elements of the justice sector (Box 4.1). Timeliness, as measured by clearance rates and disposition times, is only one element of judicial quality, alongside others such as independence, accountability, competency, integrity, transparency and public trust. In addition, adopting a broader perspective on the performance of the justice sector – such as the use and user-friendliness of alternative dispute resolution (ADRs) mechanisms or the quality and accessibility of the legal aid system – is necessary in order to measure how well the justice needs of society are addressed.

Portugal is already developing some of the elements of a more comprehensive measurement framework. Along with Estonia, Italy and Slovenia, it actively contributed to the project "Court Quality Framework Design", led by France and supported by the European Union, awarded in September 2016 for one year. The project focused on identifying indicators for court performance in three main phases:

1. Prior to submission of the claim (level of accessibility of judicial information, information on the proceedings, personalised legal consultations, etc.).
2. During the judicial proceedings (simplicity and reliability of information, communication between the courts and the parties, quality management tools).
3. After the court decision is issued (assistance to the parties, attention to the readability of court decisions, etc.).

Box 4.1. Examples of International assessment frameworks for judicial performance

Attempts at developing a detailed performance standard for justice institutions started in earnest in the 1980s. One of the most influential early reflections came from the Trial Court Performance Standards (TCPS) Project, launched in 1987 in the United States by the National Center for State Courts (NCSC) and the Bureau of Justice Assistance of the Department of Justice. The aim of the project was to elaborate "a common language to facilitate the description, classification and communication of court activities; a conceptual framework for understanding the work of courts; and, most important, a means for self-assessment, self-improvement and improved accountability". In 1990, the commission in charge of elaborating the TCPS published a set of standards, which were tested by a number of courts across several states to gauge performance and updated in 1997 to account for this experience.

There are 22 TCPS under 5 performance areas: i) access to justice; ii) expedition and timeliness; iii) equality, fairness, and integrity; iv) independence and accountability; and v) public trust and confidence. They cover aspects such as the public nature of proceedings, the convenience of use and cost of access to the court, the management of caseloads and schedules, and the representativeness of juries.

Other countries also developed frameworks for assessing court performance. In the Netherlands, for instance, the Council for the Judiciary undertook in 2002 the creation of an overarching quality system for all courts known as "RechtspraaQ", which comprises a performance measurement system applicable at the court and sectoral levels. Five areas of judicial performance are considered, each grouping several indicators: impartiality and integrity; expertise; treatment of litigants and defendants; legal unity; speed and promptness.

Initiatives were then taken to compare judicial performance across jurisdictions and to share lessons between countries. For instance, the Committee of Ministers of the Council of Europe (CoE) established the European Commission for the Efficiency of Justice (CEPEJ) in 2002 to promote the rule of law and fundamental rights in Europe, and decided to strengthen its evaluation and assistance functions in 2005 "in order to help member states to deliver justice fairly and rapidly". The toolbox that the CEPEJ has developed to this effect includes a database of judicial statistics enabling the comparison of judicial systems on efficiency, quality and effectiveness grounds, as well as a checklist for promoting the quality of justice and the courts. The CEPEJ rests its work on seven "pillars of quality" of judicial processes and decisions derived from the European Convention on Human Rights (article 6): fairness of the proceedings; reasonable duration of the proceedings; publicity of the decision and transparency of the process; protection of minors (and other subjects for whom it is appropriate to provide a form of assistance); comprehensibility of the prosecution, the course of the procedure, and decisions; right to legal assistance and access to justice in general; legal aid (when all conditions are met).

At the international level, the International Consortium for Court Excellence, which brings together bodies from various (mainly common-law) countries as well as the World Bank and the CEPEJ, proposed a Framework for Court Excellence in 2008 for application to all courts and revised and simplified it in 2013. As a normative basis, the framework lists ten values that are deemed to "guarantee due process and equal protection of the law to all those who have business before the courts, set the court culture and provide direction for all judges and staff for a proper functioning court": equality before the law, fairness, impartiality, independence of decision-making, competency, integrity, transparency, accessibility, timeliness and certainty. The framework proposes a questionnaire for courts to self-assess the extent to which these values are guiding their daily operations and a set of 11 Global Measures of Court Performance with the aim to "establish international standards and common definitions of court performance measurement that would, first, provide (…) good practices for successful performance measurement and performance management and, second, encourage comparative analysis and benchmarking across different jurisdictions".

Other approaches have considered a broader set of justice institutions than simply courts. For instance, the work of the World Bank on justice sector reforms in the 1990s addressed, in addition to the judiciary, elements such as the procedural codes, alternative dispute resolution (ADR) mechanisms, legal aid, bar associations or legal awareness education for the public. In 2012, in the context of its New Directions in Justice Reform, the World Bank proposed an even broader definition of "justice systems" encompassing "the formal and informal institutions that address breaches of law and facilitate peaceful contests over rights and obligations", including prosecutors' offices, the police, administrative enforcement mechanisms, etc.

The OECD's work on access to justice also pinpoints the variety of paths to justice, noting that "legal needs may be addressed through a range of legal and justice services (court and non-court-based), which could be arrayed along a service continuum from public legal education to early resolution services to full representation and resolution". Focusing on less than the entire justice "service continuum", by contrast, provides a partial – and possibly biased – picture of the extent to which citizens' and businesses' legal needs are satisfied.

Sources: Trial Court Performance Standards, www.ncsc.org; "RechtspraaQ", Council for the Judiciary, www.rechtspraak.nl/English/The-Council-for-the-Judiciary; European Commission for the Efficiency of Justice (CEPEJ), www.coe.int/en/web/cepej/cepej-work; International Consortium for Court Excellence, "Framework for Court Excellence" www.courtexcellence.com/; "New Directions in Justice Reform", World Bank, http://documents.worldbank.org/curated/en/928641468338516754/The-World-Bank-new-directions-in-justice-reform-a-companion-piece-to-the-updated-strategy-and-implementation-plan-on-strengthening-governance-tackling-corruption; www.oecd.org/fr/gov/access-to-justice.htm.

The Ministry of Justice is also in the process of developing a new system of indicators which would also include:

- Human, technical and budgetary resources (average cost per case, availability of the system, hours of training/per person, absenteeism rate, ration of new, completed and pending cases per person).
- Operational efficiency (productivity per magistrate, productivity per organic unit, productivity per official).
- Simplification of procedures (percentage of electronic files, automation of acts, acts per case, average number of hearings per case).
- Speed and quality (percentage of cases with more than a certain number of days, clearance rate, deviation from the statutory period).
- Court management and organisation.
- Satisfaction with services (percentage of postponement of trial hearings, satisfaction surveys, etc.).

Recent evolutions in court efficiency indicators

In terms of overall judicial performance, the data suggest that the Portuguese courts have made substantial efficiency gains, as recognised by the International Monetary Fund (IMF) in its 2018 assessment. In terms of specific results, the particular analysis of procedural times is one of the main indicators for individuals and enterprises in terms of judicial trust and access to justice. Portugal has considerably improved its court time proceedings in recent years, passing from 417 days in 2010 to 289 days in 2016 on average, according to CEPEJ data (Figure 4.1). Indeed, while Portugal compared unfavourably to other European countries until 2012, by 2016, the pendency rates and disposition times of commercial and civil courts had converged towards the averages of European countries. This means that courts have improved their efficiency by making procedural times shorter and justice prompter (e.g. the proportion of disposed case that take over five years has decreased).

For administrative and fiscal cases, Portugal's courts remain within the lower range of European countries alongside Cyprus,[5] Greece, Italy and Malta.

Figure 4.1. Disposition times in courts of first instance in 2010 and 2016

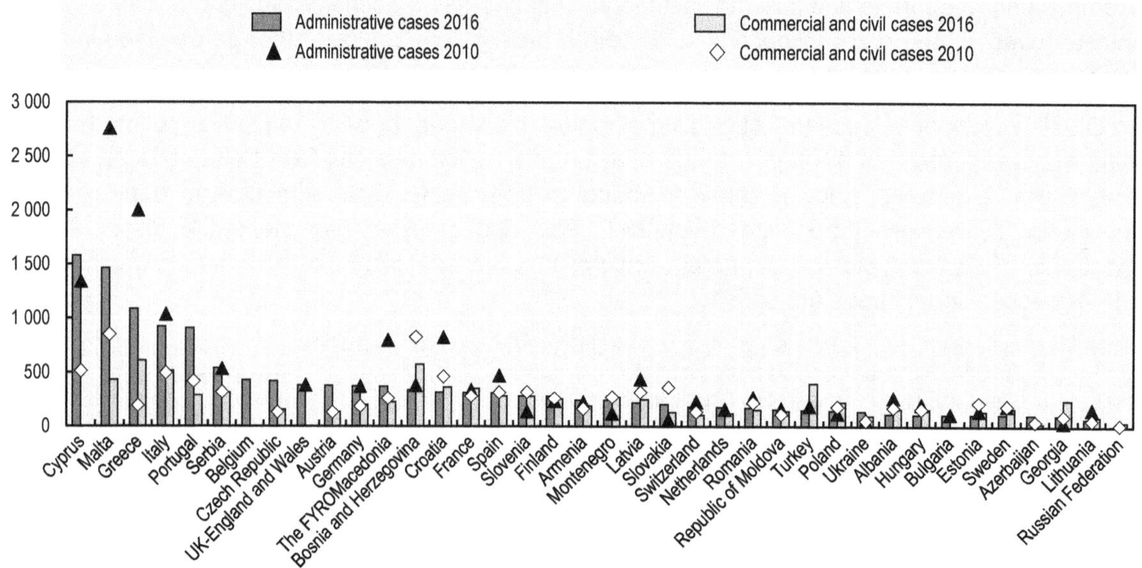

Note by Turkey: The information in this document with reference to "Cyprus" relates to the southern part of the Island. There is no single authority representing both Turkish and Greek Cypriot people on the Island. Turkey recognises the Turkish Republic of Northern Cyprus (TRNC). Until a lasting and equitable solution is found within the context of the United Nations, Turkey shall preserve its position concerning the "Cyprus issue".

Note by all the European Union Member States of the OECD and the European Union: The Republic of Cyprus is recognised by all members of the United Nations with the exception of Turkey. The information in this document relates to the area under the effective control of the Government of the Republic of Cyprus.

Note: Ratio between the number of pending cases and the average number of resolved cases per day during the year, i.e. the number of days needed for the court to resolve all pending cases at the current pace.

Source: CEPEJ (2018), "European judicial systems – Efficiency and quality of justice", *CEPEJ Studies*, No. 26. European Commission for the Efficiency of Justice, Council of Europe.

The improvement in measured performance has been particularly marked in the area of enforcement, where clearance rates have consistently exceeded 100% since 2013, leading to a dramatic reduction in the number of pending cases (Figure 4.2).

It appears that the increase in the clearance rate has been largely caused by a fall in the number of new cases filed, which has been below 150 000 cases on average per year since 2016, against close to 350 000 in 2012. The number of disposed cases has also decreased during the period, from close to 330 000 in 2012 to slightly more than 250 000 on annual average in 2016-18.

Furthermore, it should be noted that a substantial part of the improvement observed since 2013 may stem from several changes introduced by the new Code of Civil Procedure (see Chapter 2, Box 2.1 on the Civil Procedure reform). In particular, the dispositions regarding the termination of proceedings and the closing of certain enforcement cases have likely resulted in a reduction of several hundreds of thousands in the number of pending cases.

These changes also seem to have contributed to the sudden hike in the average duration of enforcement cases and in the percentage of cases with a duration of more than five years in 2013, followed by a decline in 2014 (Figure 4.3). The steady increase in both indicators since the end of 2014 is, however, a matter of concern as it might indicate a "hard core" of cases for which efficiency gains have not taken place.

Figure 4.2. Clearance rates and pendency for enforcement cases

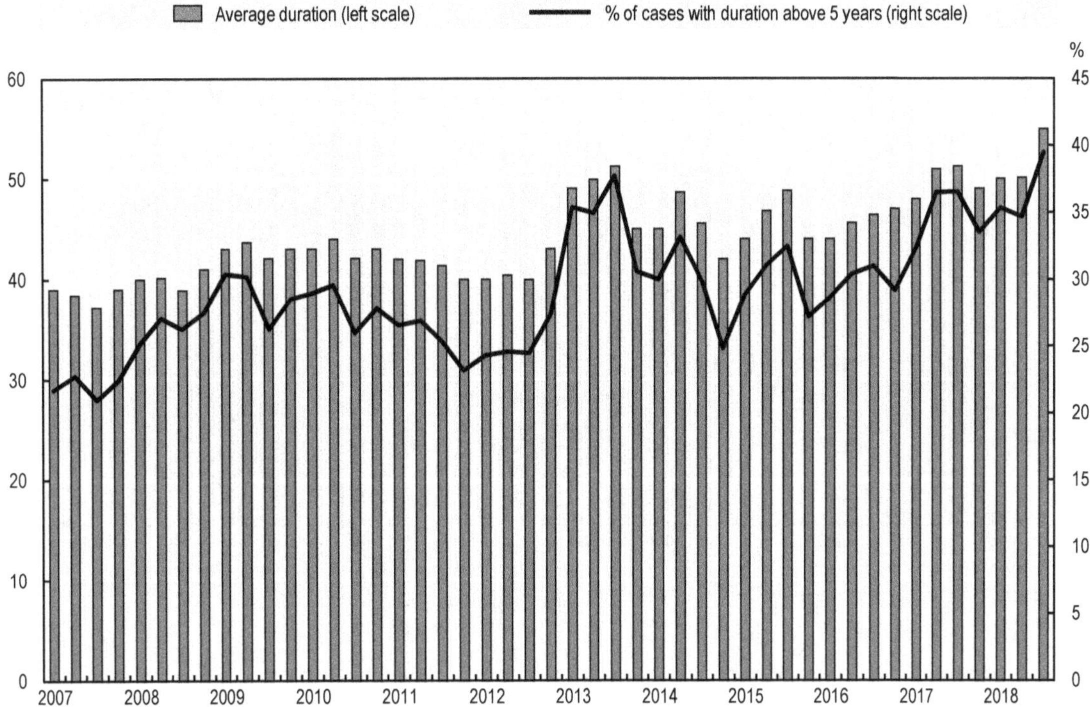

Source: Data provided by the Ministry of Justice, DGPJ statistics, https://estatisticas.justica.gov.pt.

Figure 4.3. The duration of enforcement cases

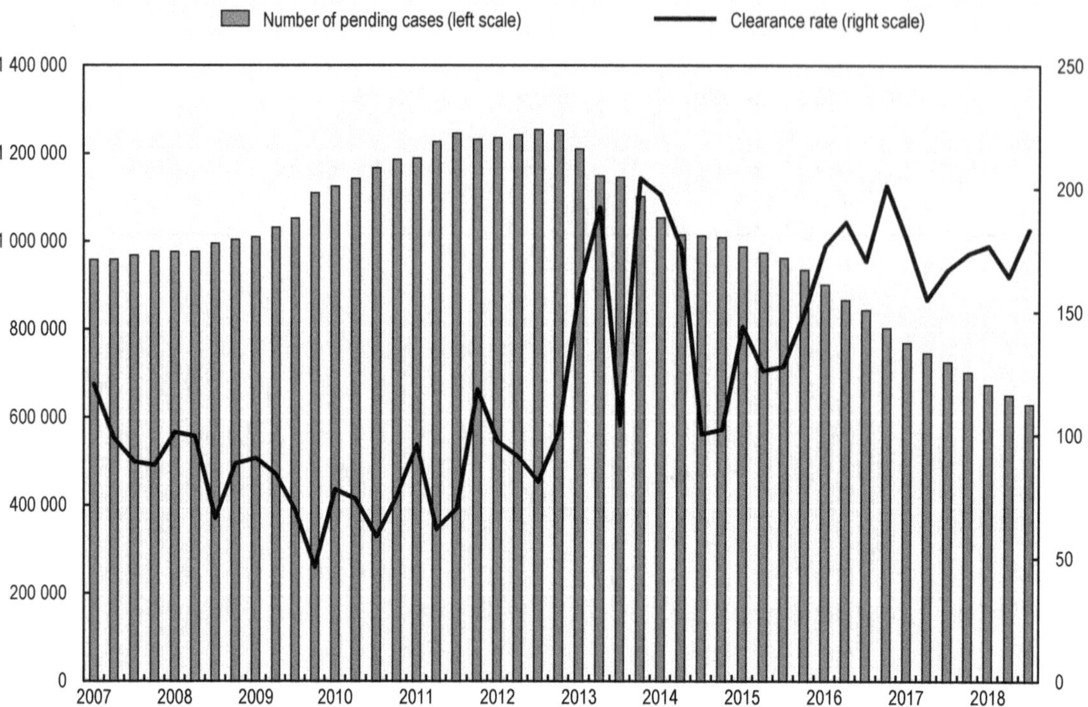

Source: Data provided by the Ministry of Justice, DGPJ statistics, https://estatisticas.justica.gov.pt.

Figure 4.4 provides an indication of the evolution of efficiency in other courts, as measured by the clearance rate. It appears that other courts – which were not directly impacted by the new Code of Civil Procedure dispositions on pendency – have not experienced an increase in clearance rates similar to that of courts of first instance.

Figure 4.4. Clearance rates in Portugal's courts

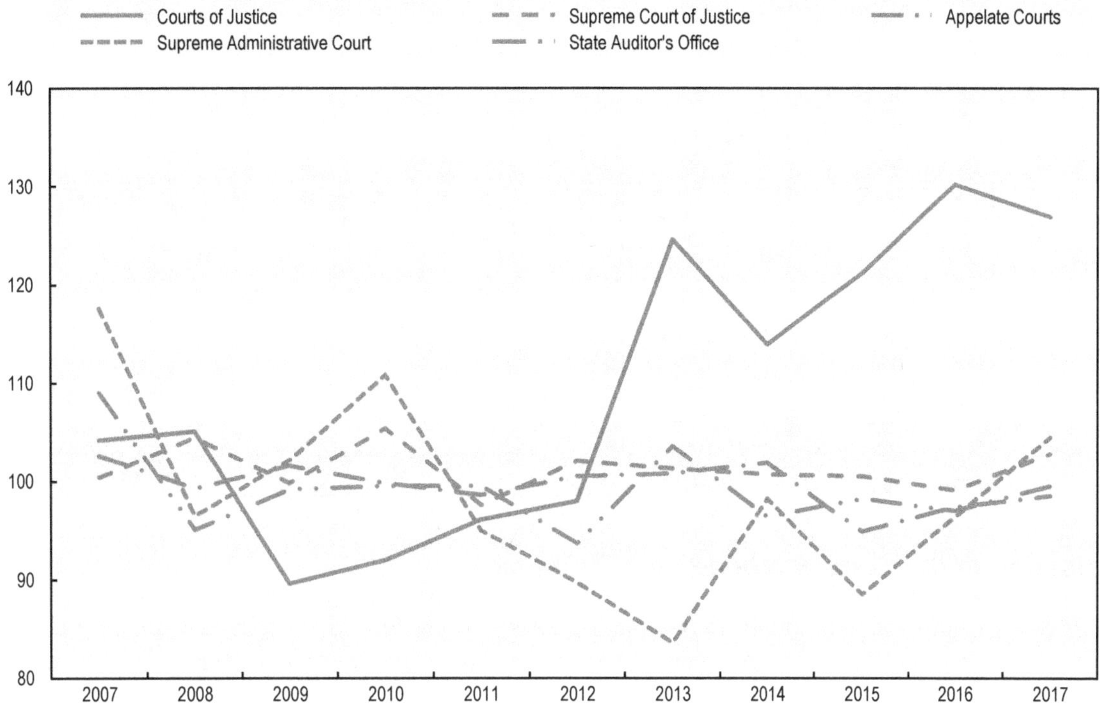

Note: Ratio between the number of disposed cases and the number of new cases during the year.
Source: Data provided by the Ministry of Justice, DGPJ statistics.

In summary, while the dramatic rise in the clearance rate and drop in pendency of enforcement cases in civil and commercial courts of first instance is *per se* a positive development, these results would need to be interpreted with caution. First, they stem from a reduction in the filing of new cases, not an increase in the number of disposed cases. Second, they are partly related to a change in the method of accounting of pendency. Third, average durations of cases have increased in recent years. Finally, other courts (administrative, appellate, Supreme Courts, State Auditor's office) have not experienced similar improvements.

More granular longitudinal data (e.g. broken down according to the complexity of cases) would be needed in order to fully assess the impacts of different changes introduced as part of the recent reforms and have a better understanding of the efficiency of Portugal's courts.

Portugal has also seen an evolution of trust in justice systems over the past several years (Figure 4.5). Yet, trial length in Portugal is still seen as long when compared to other OECD countries whose average number is 221.36. Over 35% of cases still take more than 1 year to resolve (OECD, 2019). Recently, in the area of enforcement, the number of completed cases has consistently exceeded cases entering the system (whose number has been declining since the crisis years) along with the processing times. Yet, it would be important for Portugal to continue its efforts to improve the resolution of enforcement cases, including contract enforcement and insolvency proceedings, as they are essential for businesses.

Importantly, care is needed in attributing specific improvements to individual initiatives. Moreover, indicators such as trial length may also be affected by behavioural conditions and incentives of different actors, including culture, socioeconomic characteristics, business fluctuations, substantive law, as well as costs and rules, lawyer's incentives, ADR and legal certainty, which calls for a holistic approach to justice reforms.

Figure 4.5. Evolution of trust in EU Justice system, 2014 - 2018

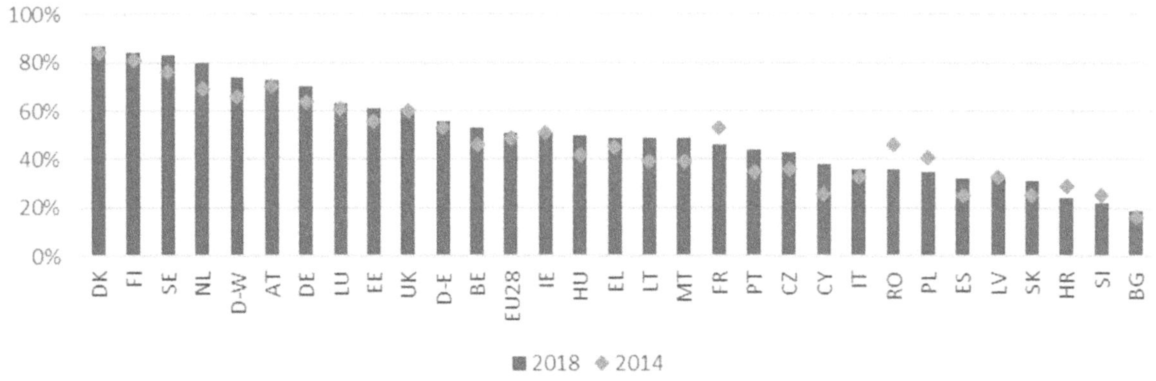

Sources: European Commission (2018), "Public opinion in the European Union", *Standard Eurobarometer 90*, Vol. A: Countries, http://data.europa.eu/euodp/en/data/dataset/S2215_90_3_STD90_ENG; European Commission (2018), "Public opinion in the European Union", *Standard Eurobarometer 82*, Vol. A: Countries, http://data.europa.eu/euodp/en/data/dataset/S2215_90_3_STD90_ENG.

Evaluation of the costs and benefits of Tribunal +

The Ministry of Justice has sought to assess the effect of the Justiça + Próxima plan, with particular emphasis on the total costs and benefits of Tribunal +. An *ex ante* evaluation based on the results of the Sintra pilot project was conducted at the end of 2017 (Ministry of Justice of Portugal, 2018).[6] An interim and a final evaluation of Tribunal + are also planned in the course of 2019.

The *ex ante* study concludes that the estimated costs of Tribunal + would be close to EUR 14 million of start-up investment costs and EUR 2.4 million of operational costs per year, while its expected benefits would reach EUR 69.6 million per year. The bulk of these benefits stems from an estimated gain of 3 300 clerical positions (in full-time equivalents) in both back-office and front-office functions. Additional gains are related to the costs saved by users in their interactions with the courts, in terms of both direct costs (reduced travel) and opportunity costs (time saved). Non-monetary benefits include an estimated reduction of 320 000 in the number of pending cases at the national level.

As usual for this type of studies, the cost-benefit analysis of Tribunal + is based on data provided by the implementing entities (the Ministry of Justice for the cost figures, the consultancy in charge of the re-engineering of back-office workflows in Sintra for data on efficiency gains in carrying out individual tasks). The study then extrapolates from this data under various modelling assumptions. For instance, productivity gains in the performance of individual clerical tasks are simply added and assumed to generate proportional cost savings and backlog reductions. Yet such an assumption may overlook the possibility of efficiency losses and bottlenecks at other points in the judicial process.

An example of possible bottlenecks could be enforcement action falling under the responsibility of enforcement agents outside the court. Indeed, preliminary estimates by the Ministry of Justice indicate that less than 15% of enforcement cases are pending on a decision or an action by judges and clerks;[7] the bulk of pending case are awaiting action by the parties, third parties or an external enforcement agent, or the expiry of a period.[8]

More generally, when updating the evaluation of Tribunal +, it would be important to take proper account of the dampening effects that could be caused by: i) losses of efficiency in the implementation of new work processes at the court level; and ii) other capacity constraints and bottlenecks in the management of cases.

In terms of the evaluation process, potential improvement areas include submitting *ex ante* evaluations to an independent review and a formal *ex post* assessment based on monitoring data.

The *ex post* evaluation of Tribunal +, based on observed outcomes at the court level, will help to establish a clear picture of the improvements introduced by the project and the obstacles that it has faced.

A common method for analysing the impact of a project such as Tribunal + on court efficiency is to compare the *evolution* of efficiency indicators in courts that have participated in the project to that of courts that have not.[9] The fact that Tribunal + was carried out as a pilot project at different times in different courts offers an opportunity for such a comparative analysis.

In application of this method, Figures 4.6 and 4.7 below compare the evolution of clearance rates and numbers of disposed cases[10] in the court of Sintra, where the original pilot project was implemented from the fall of 2016 onwards, in courts of the West Lisbon Comarca, where the pilot project was launched in the fall of 2017, and in other courts in the country where the project was not implemented during the period under review (or not advanced to the point of influencing the indicators). To facilitate the comparison of evolutions since the start of the project, all values are expressed as indexes with a base value of 100 in the fourth quarter of 2016.

Figure 4.6. Clearance rates in courts implementing Tribunal +

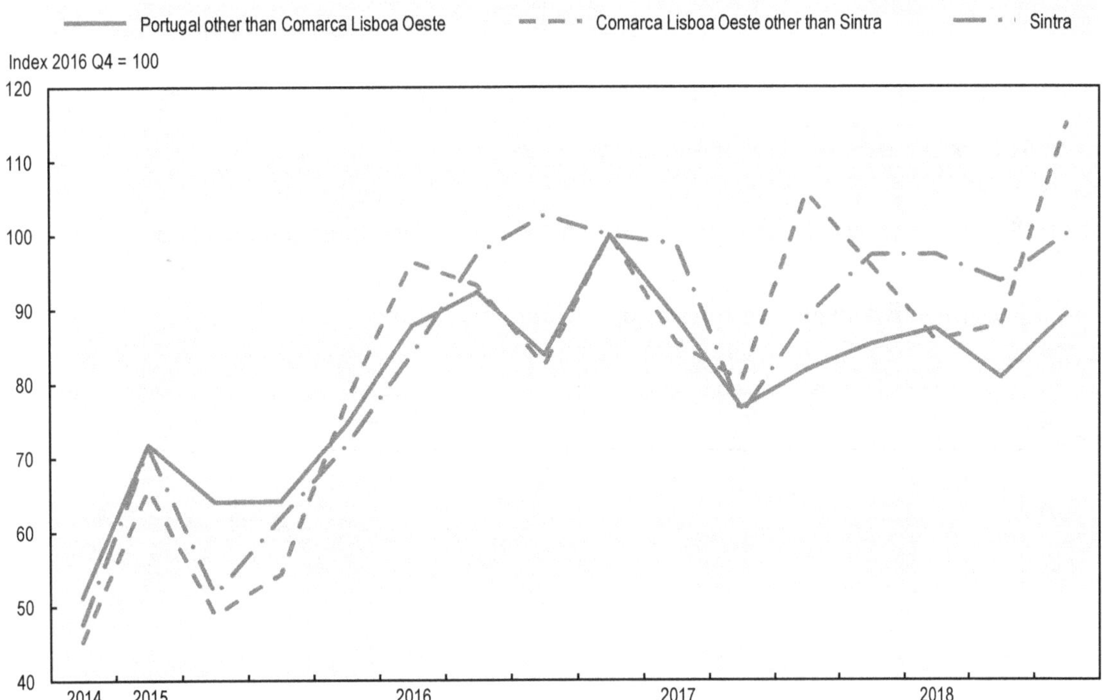

Note: Ratio between the number of disposed cases and the number of new cases during each quarter.
Source: Data provided by the Ministry of Justice, DGPJ statistics.

Figure 4.7. Number of disposed cases in courts implementing Tribunal +

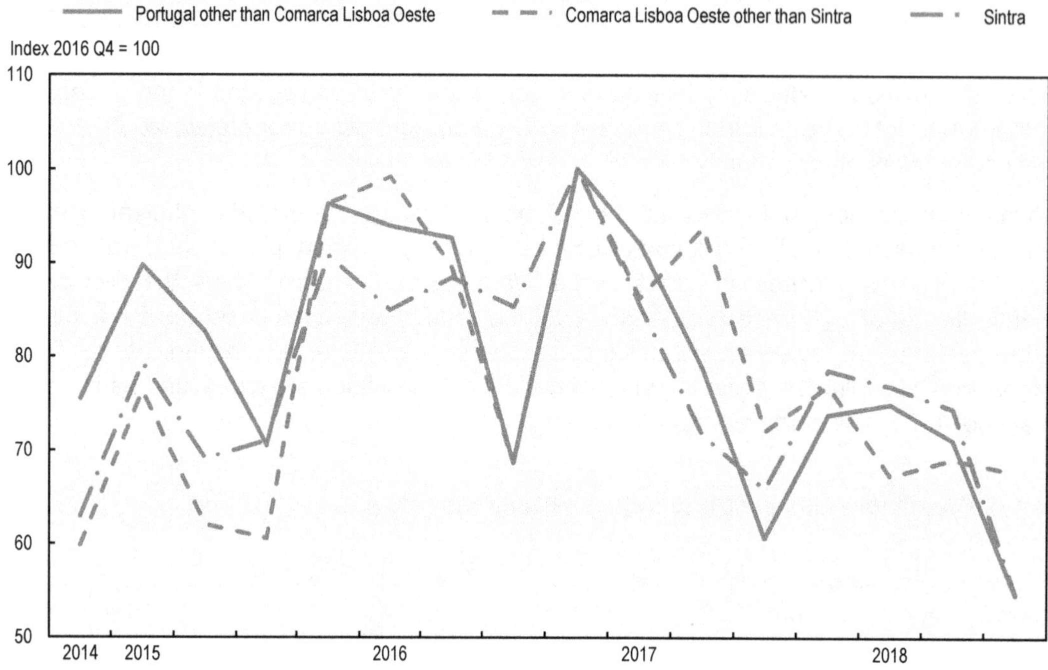

Source: Data provided by the Ministry of Justice, DGPJ statistics.

Similarly, Figure 4.8 shows the evolution of disposition times in the three groups of courts.

Figure 4.8. Disposition times in courts implementing Tribunal +

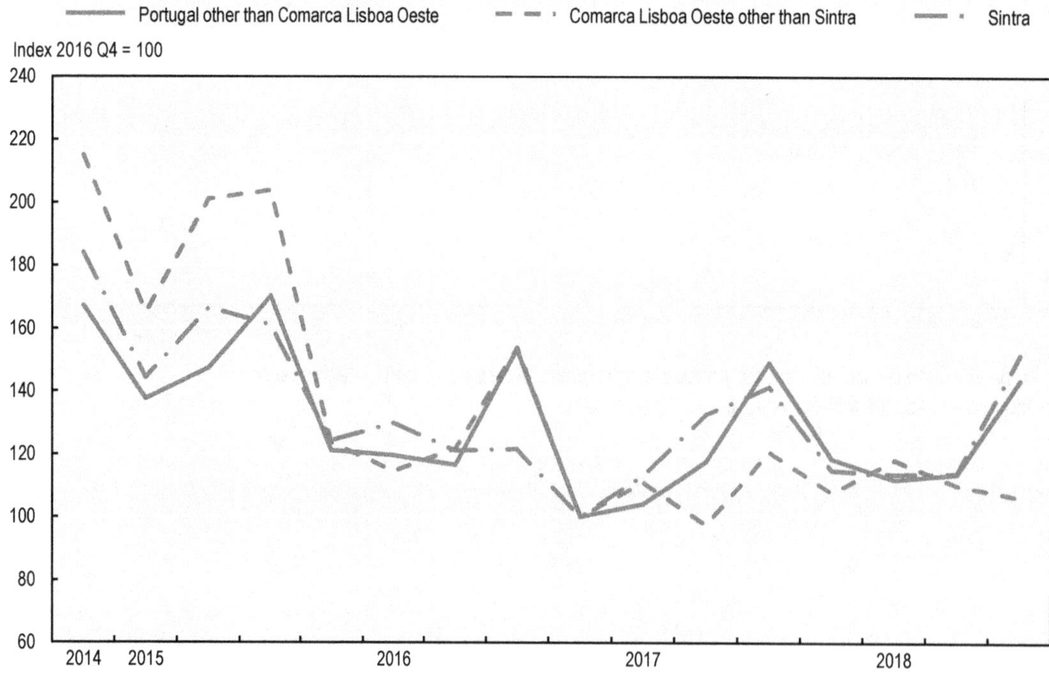

Note: Ratio between the number of pending cases and the average number of resolved cases per day during the quarter, i.e. the number of days needed for the court to resolve all pending cases at the current pace.
Source: Data provided by the Ministry of Justice, DGPJ statistics.

Several observations can be made when comparing the results of the three groups of courts:

1. Clearance rates were following an upward trend in all the reviewed courts until the end of 2016. They deteriorated during the first half of 2017 – a slump might have to do with a gradual fading of the effects of the 2013-14 reforms but have somewhat improved since. The increase since the second quarter of 2017 has been slightly stronger in Sintra than in Portuguese courts outside of the Western Lisbon Comarca but lower than in other courts of the Comarca.
2. The improvements in clearance rates between the second quarter of 2017 and the third quarter of 2018 appear to be largely due to a fall in the number of new cases. The number of disposed cases, which was following a positive trend until the end of 2016, is since on a downward path. The evolution in the number of disposed cases has been identical in the court of Sintra and in Portuguese courts outside of the Western Lisbon Comarca, which did not implement Tribunal + during the period.
3. Disposition times were on a downward trend until the end of 2016. They have since stabilised in the courts of the Western Lisbon Comarca other than Sintra, while they increased by more than 40% in the court of Sintra and in other courts of the country.

The analysis shows that at this early stage it could be difficult to fully identify a full range of effects of Tribunal + on the courts in which it has been implemented as a pilot project due to a number of factors.

First, micro-level efficiency gains might take more time to translate into an improvement in court-level indicators. More detailed indicators might help to monitor such delays in the diffusion of efficiency gains.

In terms of methodology, this points to the relevance of a full representation of case management processes – including the work of judges and prosecutors alongside that of clerks – as a basis for the evaluation and monitoring of effects. Such a representation would facilitate the identification of potential bottlenecks and efficiency losses. In terms of the evaluation process, potential improvement areas include submitting *ex ante* evaluations to an independent review and a formal *ex post* assessment based on monitoring data.

Second, the measures reviewed in the previous sections, in particular the adoption of a new Code of Civil Procedure, the creation of the district clusters and the changes it has induced in terms of court management and specialisation, can be expected to have far-reaching effects on the organisation of work, labour productivity and efficiency in handling cases. The direct impact of the new code on court pendency rates has already been mentioned. The monitoring framework for Tribunal + could seek to assess and isolate the influence of external factors on court performance.

Third, it should be emphasised that an important part of the benefits of Tribunal + resides in an improvement of outcomes other than macro-level efficiency, in particular increases in user satisfaction and in transparency. The monitoring framework for Tribunal + should also seek to identify and measure such outcomes.

These observations point to the necessity of elaborating a general analytical framework for ensuring that the evaluation and monitoring of Tribunal + are both consistent and comprehensive. The management of the project would benefit from the elaboration of a detailed logical framework (or theory of change) that would spell out the causal linkages between its key measures and their direct and indirect outcomes and ultimate impact. Figure 4.9 presents the sketch of a theory of change for the Tribunal + measures. A (more) detailed logical framework could be used to identify and assess external factors that could potentially influence outcomes, locate possible bottlenecks for efficiency gains, and orient methodological and data collection choices in future monitoring and evaluation activities.

Such a framework would help to further and complement the analysis presented above by more detailed investigations and further statistical observations.

Figure 4.9. A tentative theory of change for the Tribunal + project

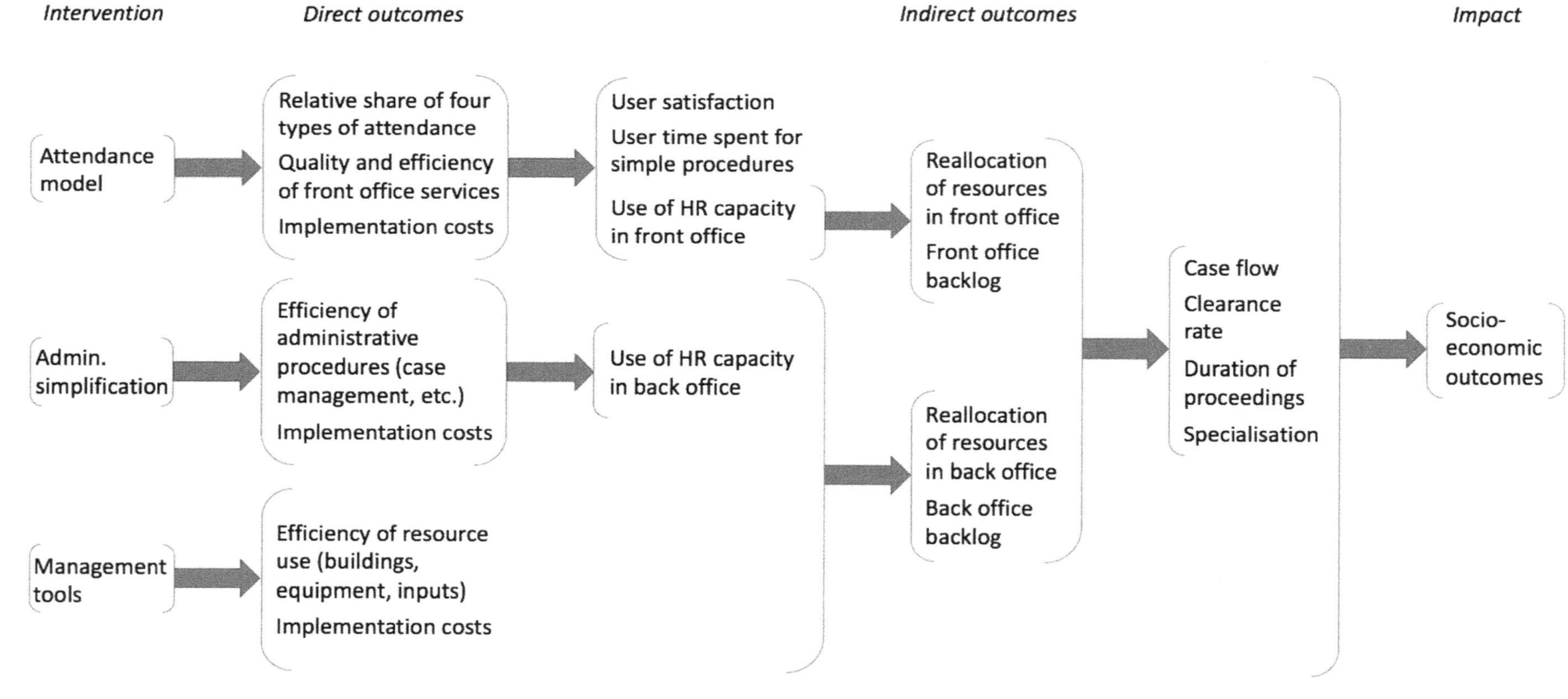

Stakeholder assessments of Tribunal +

An important achievement of the reforms is to be appreciated by the judiciary staff, by lawyers and by court users. The OECD has carried out interviews with lawyers, judges, prosecutors and, in general, there is a consensus that the introduction of new information technology (IT) tools (in particular the new version of the Citius case management system), the new organisation of back offices and the new attendance model Balcão +, are positive steps that substantially improve the functioning of courts – although some improvements appear to be warranted. From the broader citizen perspective, many reported that they would still need to come to court to obtain most information.

According to the clerks who were involved in the re-engineering of work processes in the court of Sintra, the measure did not only lead to important efficiency gains; it also had a transformative effect on the type of tasks that they routinely perform. The new organisational template implemented in Sintra was based on a minute examination of the work of clerks and the selection of appropriate tools to enhance their efficiency, in combination with improved IT systems. One of the consequences was to reduce the number of purely administrative tasks in which judges have to be involved. This has increased the autonomy of the clerks and allowed the judges to focus more on adjudicatory work. The changes also allowed achieving a reduction in the pendency of intermediary decisions by judges, thus increasing the number of judicial acts with a final decision.

The measure has the potential to have similar effects in each of the 22 other court clusters, provided that:

- The same degree of care is applied when implementing the template in order to take proper account of the specific conditions and constraints of each case.
- The clerical staff and the magistrates have the same level of commitment to the implementation of the new scheme.

The reforms are also positively evaluated by the judges interviewed in the course of this review. The new version of the Citius platform, in which lawyers send their petitions electronically at the start of a case, enables them to better plan their work and be more efficient with the use of their time. They also perceive that digitalisation and the re-organisation of clerical work lead to a more efficient workflow. Thanks to Balcão +, hearings in court start in a smoother manner and with much fewer delays than before.

However, the judges consider that to fully reap the benefits of the new organisation, some of the needs that it has engendered will have to be addressed. These concern:

- Training for the judges to fully exploit the capacity of the new information system.
- Further improvement of the new information system: Citius was initially developed with the aim to simplify clerical work routines through digitalisation; it was extended to the work of judges and prosecution at a later stage, but some design flaws remain. For instance, a judge or a public prosecutor cannot open a case and modify it without the prior intervention of a clerk.
- A formal instruction by the High Council of the Judiciary to judges to use clerical capacities differently.
- Human resources: the judges pinpoint that the reform has revived a structural deficit of the Portuguese judiciary in paralegal staff who can assist magistrates on substantive matters (such as verifying the jurisprudence) and by making the interface with the clerks.

For the lawyers, the reform has essentially modified the conditions in which they interact with the judiciary, from their physical access to the courts to the use of Citius as a unique channel for submitting their request and documentation and receiving notifications. Their assessment of these changes is positive both on behalf of their clients and on their own, but the lawyers also indicate several areas in which adjustments and improvement are warranted:

- Some tasks have been transferred from the courts to the lawyers as a consequence of the reform, e.g. digitalising documents or collecting information on the parties. The introduction of the new civil procedural code in 2013 had already caused a similar shift (e.g. on the responsibility to summon witnesses in civil cases).
- Certain legal means of identification (including driver's licences, or residence permits for foreigners) are no longer considered valid to access the courts.
- The proofs of presence in the court provided to users do not list all the information required by their employers.
- Lawyers have to take a separate ticket for every file on which they are working.
- There is a lack of clarity concerning the lawyers' right to access all clerical services, which should be maintained.

Businesses confirm that online services are a greatly welcomed reform that should facilitate the accessibility of justice. Greater communication on these reforms will enable better familiarity with the introduced changes. Yet they also underline the importance of addressing the complexity of laws and regulations, frequent changes in the legislation, backlogs and cost of access.

As testified by these reactions, the reforms introduced as part of the Justiça + Próxima plan and the Tribunal + project constitute an important modernisation package for the Portuguese judiciary. The fact that the key measures have been designed and implemented in dialogue with some stakeholders and that they are appreciated by the judicial staff and the users will contribute to maximising their impact and ensuring their sustainability.

However, complementary measures would be needed in order to reap the full benefits of the reforms in terms of court efficiency and – even more – of performance of the justice sector in general.

The reforms undertaken as part of Tribunal + initiative have so far focused on sectors under the direct responsibility of the Ministry of Justice; in particular, they have not directly addressed the work of judges. This has two important implications for the impact of past and ongoing reforms. First, part of the efficiency gains made in clerical tasks might be lost due to capacity constraints in judicial decision-making. Second, the emergence of new models of work organisation in the courts, which relies on strong co-operation between the judges and the clerks, might be hampered by the limited involvement of the former. To succeed, the reforms, therefore, need to enter a new phase in which the High Council of the Judiciary and the judiciary at large play an active role in assessing and improving the adjudication process.

Further progress is also needed in the administrative and fiscal courts where, according to diverse stakeholders, efficiency is hampered by excessive formalism and less than adequate support staff (particularly in courts of first instance). Simplification and strengthening of human resources in support functions beyond the Supreme Court (i.e. legal clerks, assistant judges) appear to be the solutions to address backlogs and improve both efficiency and quality. In addition, while systematisation of the clerks' work can allow gaining in court efficiency, it is important to maintain flexibility for clerks to respond to arising needs.

The monitoring and evaluation framework for Justiça + Próxima

The Ministry of Justice has also developed a common framework to monitor progress in the implementation of all measures included in Justiça + Próxima. The entity or person responsible for each measure reports monthly on development and/or implementation, on the achievement of target indicators and objectives, and on cost. By the end of July 2019, the monitoring indicated that 184 measures had been approved within the framework of the plan, representing a total investment of EUR 42 million. Of these, 95 are reported to be concluded and 64 under implementation (Figure 4.10).

Figure 4.10. Measures concluded vs. development of Justiça + Próxima

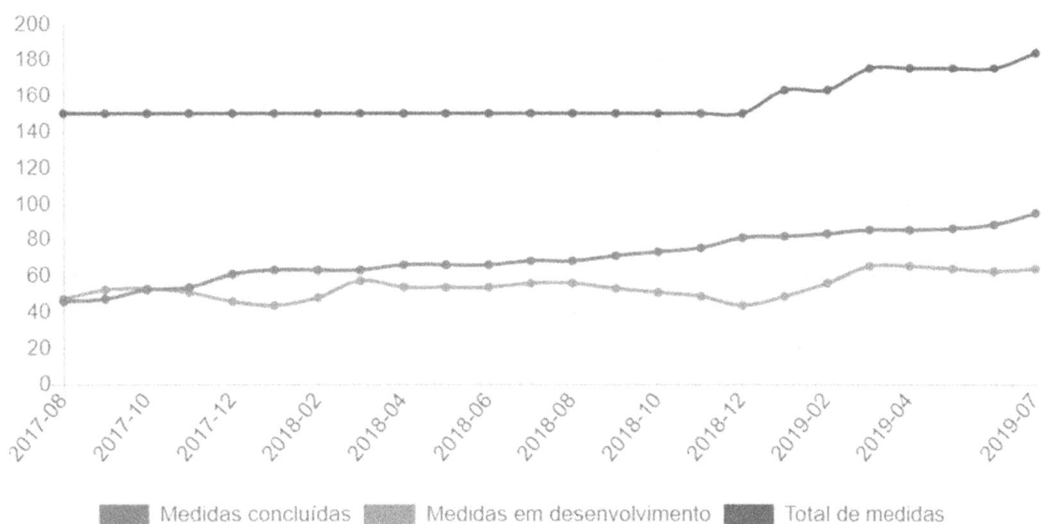

Source: Data and statistics of the Portuguese Justice system's official website: Portuguese Justice System (2019), *Medidas concluídas vs desenvolvimento do Plano Justiça mais Próxima*, https://partilha.justica.gov.pt/Transparencia/Dados-e-Estatisticas/-Medidas-concluidas-vs-execucao-do-Plano-Justica-mais-Proxima.

The assessment of the effects of other measures in the Justiça + Próxima plan usually focuses on direct savings of operational costs (e.g. savings on the cost of post stamps) and human resources. As in the case of the Tribunal + evaluation, the latter are estimated by extrapolating time savings by task to full-time equivalents, which might similarly overlook sources of efficiency loss.

The ministry has not published a global estimate of the benefits of these measures. However, the sum of its evaluations for individual effects exceeds EUR 15 million per year, to be added to the EUR 69.6 million of Tribunal +.

Indicators and objectives mainly focus on the steps of the development and implementation process, with the exception of the measures included in Tribunal +, for which certain outcome-related indicators have been defined (Table 4.1).

Table 4.1. Outcome indicators for Tribunal +

Outcome	Indicator
Labour productivity in courts	Total gains in terms of full-time equivalent (FTE) jobs
	Percentage of FTE gains for court officials
	Percentage of FTE gains for magistrates
	Number of total FTE gains per area
	Percentage of total FTE gains per area
Overall efficiency of courts	Number of pending cases
	Resolution rate (percentage of new cases completed)

Source: Ministry of Justice of Portugal (2018), "Monitoring the consolidation process on the implementation of the pilot-scheme Tribunal + and roll out preparation at national level'", Tribunal + project document.

While the current indicators cover the main categories of benefits identified as a result of the implementation of Tribunal +, it would be important to explicitly integrate aspects that are beyond the organisational boundaries of the courts, such as user satisfaction, trust in justice institutions and citizens' broader access to justice.

In interviews, several stakeholders involved in the decision-making process for the Tribunal + project indicated that one of the important – albeit less tangible – goals of the project was to improve court user experiences and the perception of justice institutions in society. When monitoring the effects of the project, it would, therefore, be useful to seek to integrate these aspects.

Finally, as already noted in the case of Tribunal +, it would be important to design of a general analytical framework for ensuring that the evaluation and monitoring of measures in the Justiça + Próxima plan are both consistent and comprehensive. The Ministry of Justice would benefit from the elaboration of a detailed logical framework similar to the one sketched in Figure 4.9 above for all of the important measures – or clusters of measures – in the plan.

Towards effective scaling up of Tribunal +

Effective planning of the scaling-up process is an important component of the expansion and institutionalisation of justice innovations and modernisation efforts. One of the key challenges in scaling up is that special organisational, financial and human resources are mobilised for the pilot phase, but are not available to the same extent during the rollout phase. As a result, scaling up is often handicapped by the lack of resources, weak capacities and limited ownership. This requires careful balancing of efforts to build capacities, ensure ownership of the reform by a wide range of stakeholders and develop institutionalisation strategies (WHO, 2010).

The Ministry of Justice has identified several main risks of the rollout project to be addressed: i) the need to ensure adequate co-ordination between all entities involved in the project; ii) the need to ensure that the speeding up of registry tasks does not represent a constraint for the workload of judges; iii) disparity in terms of the availability of equipment, which necessitated a phased and gradual approach to the implementation.

To address these risks, the rollout of the pilot project is scheduled to take place in a gradual manner to accommodate local needs and capacities (both in terms of skills, resources and infrastructure). Courts have been categorised and innovations will be implemented according to the selected courts and adapted to their needs (Box 4.2).

The Ministry of Justice reports developing a number of planning and monitoring tools, such as a rollout activity planning and reporting process, use of selected indicators (on court efficiency, efficiency of human resources [e.g. the amount of time gained for court clerks and judges] and on the expansion of the project [e.g. courts that have benefitted from the intervention]), as well as risk matrix and mitigation plans.

In order to increase awareness about the project and address resistance to change, the change management plan for the project also provides for communication tools, such as: the Tribunal + newsletter; press releases and general information on the public portals (e.g. justiça.gov.pt, justicamaisproxima.mj.pt, portugal.gov.pt) issued on a regular basis; a flyer explaining the project to users, etc. Indeed, lessons learned from making reform happen in OECD countries underline the fundamental importance of regular communication.

In parallel, steps to increase the capacity of courts to implement scaling up are being taken (e.g. upgrading court infrastructure, clerks training with the involvement of the Kaizen Institute, identifying champions for rollout in 23 clusters, etc.)

Some of the ongoing challenges include increasing the resource team's capacity to support scaling up and ongoing strategic choices to support vertical (institutionalisation) and horizontal (expansion/replication) scaling up.

Box 4.2. The current approach to rolling out Tribunal +

Back-office efficiency – through the implementation of the Kaizen methodology for the clerk work process in 23 court clusters. The implementation of the methodology involved delivering training to clerks in all clusters (how to organise daily activities, etc.) and continuous monitoring. "Train the trainers" modules have been developed and implemented as part of the training centre for clerks under the General Directorate of Justice Administration (DGAJ). The trained team leads will engage and train clerk teams in individual courts to implement Kaizen methodologies in 2019. Currently, 23 process units use the Kaizen work organisation methodology and 20 jurisdictions (*Comarcas*) work with the new office organisation method in 74 buildings.

Front office – the rollout of the new attendance model depends on the availability of the equipment and technology and is scheduled to be implemented in 44 courts by the end of the year. In 2019 and 2020, the attendance model will be rolled out to an additional 55 and 180 courts respectively (large and medium). The single counter for properties, project Balcão +, is now operational in 48 courts. Likewise, from 1st September 2016 to 12 February 2019, the attendance tickets and automatic presence declarations issued amounted 218 888 and 27 163 respectively.

These measures represent EUR 15 208 232 (of which EUR 5 749 000 have been already invested). The total budget from European funds such as SAMA (*Sistema De Apoio À Transformação Digital Da Administração Pública*), European Social Fund and the Justice Modernisation Fund (FMJ) amounts to EUR 3.5 million and the total Portuguese state budget – OE (*Orçamento de Estado*) represents EUR 11.7 million

Some associated projects include:

1. Online criminal record certificates (*Certificados do Registo Criminal*). This programme, launched in July 2016, has issued 106 026 certificates and data from 2017 and 2018 shows that online channel usage increased by 85%. The first semester of 2019 also shows that more than 20% of criminal records issued for companies were issued online. All in all, the access code was used 300 000 times.
2. Online court case consultation. Implemented in May 2017, data up to November 2018 showed that court cases were accessed 22 035 times and 60% of access occurs during out-of-office hours.
3. Alerts sent to lawyers and solicitors, including various notifications, have been operational since July 2016. The number of messages and/or emails sent for those purposes amounted to 136 534 and 70% of users already work under this system.
4. Language simplification in notifications has been applied since June 2017 and notifications sent 302 226 times. The first year of application shows that the number of injunctions where the person paid the debt when receiving notifications increased by 50%.
5. Electronic judicial certificates. Issued since July 2017, the number of online certificates amounts to 41 949, 27% of which were issued without human intervention (automatic/instant). The access code shows this programme has been used 29 000 times.

Source: Data provided by the Ministry of Justice of Portugal, 2019.

Furthermore, ensuring the sustainability of reform efforts requires paying attention to policy institutionalisation, internal regulations, budgets and other dimensions of the justice system. As such, appropriate institutions should be involved in making the transition from decision to implementation (OECD, 2010). To this end, it would be important to continue actively engaging the administration of the Ministry of Justice (i.e. the DGAJ), which is responsible for the organisation and management of courts, including the non-judicial workforce (e.g. clerks), budgets, and information technology (IT), equipment, etc. The DGAJ is also responsible for training non-judicial officers, such as clerks, through the designated training centre and organisation of court workflows. Another important institution actively involved is the Institute for Financial Management and Justice Equipment (IGFEJ), which is responsible for the IT system and equipment in the justice sector and will be overseeing the technical capacity of the courts to implement the new model. In fact, it would be important that both the DGAJ and IGFEJ have a full leading role in the management of both the rollout, implementation and monitoring of the programme.

In addition, international experience underlines the importance of ongoing political leadership and involvement in the success of reforms. As such, in line with the project evaluation, it would be beneficial if the expansion of Tribunal + could be accompanied by the establishment of a dedicated structure in charge of the management and monitoring of the programme's various aspects. This would help facilitate and accelerate implementation by transferring knowledge, capacity and ownership to the administration while ensuring continuity and taking into account lessons learned from pilot projects.

Such a structure could involve setting up a management and monitoring committee, which could be composed of the Secretary of State for Justice (the executive sponsor of the project and the head of the committee), the Justice Assistant Secretary of State, and representatives from the DGAJ, the Secretary of State for Justice Cabinet and the IGFEJ. The co-ordination of the team for the management of change programme, according to the usual activities that come under their jurisdictions, could also be assigned to the Secretary of State for Justice Cabinet, DGAJ and IGFEJ (Box 4.3).

Box 4.3. Proposed management model

In line with the project evaluation, the proposed management model could reflect the following roles and responsibilities (Figure 4.11):

- Secretary of State for Justice – Executive sponsor of the programme, given that the administrative simplification and information system areas are under his/her responsibility. The Justice Secretary of State could chair the proposed Management and Monitoring Committee.
- Office of the Justice Secretary of State – Represented by a person responsible for the overall co-ordination of the programme and represented in the Management and Monitoring Committee. This person may be assisted by other specialists in specific technical areas.
- Management and Monitoring Committee – a new unit, potentially under the office of the Justice Secretary of State – responsible for managing and monitoring the overall rollout and implementation of the programme. The Management and Monitoring Committee is also responsible and its decision is binding.
- Directorate-General for Justice Administration (DGAJ) – Represented in the Monitoring Committee, in the co-ordination of the programme management team and technical managers in areas under their responsibility (e.g. training, tenders, etc.).
- Institute for Financial Management and Justice Equipment (IGFEJ) - Represented in the Monitoring Committee, in the co-ordination of the programme management team and technical managers in areas under their responsibility (e.g. information systems, infrastructures, equipment, tenders, etc.).

Source: Based on the information provided by the Government of Portugal and adapted by the OECD.

An advisory committee, with no decision-making powers, composed of representatives from the High Council of the Judiciary, the High Council for Public Prosecution, the High Council for the Administrative and Fiscal Courts, the Council of Court Clerks, and representatives of Higher Courts, could also be set up.

The establishment of this dedicated structure could enable the participation of main stakeholder and, help ensure continuity and knowledge transfer from current pilot projects under Tribunal +.

Figure 4.11. Current roles and responsibilities

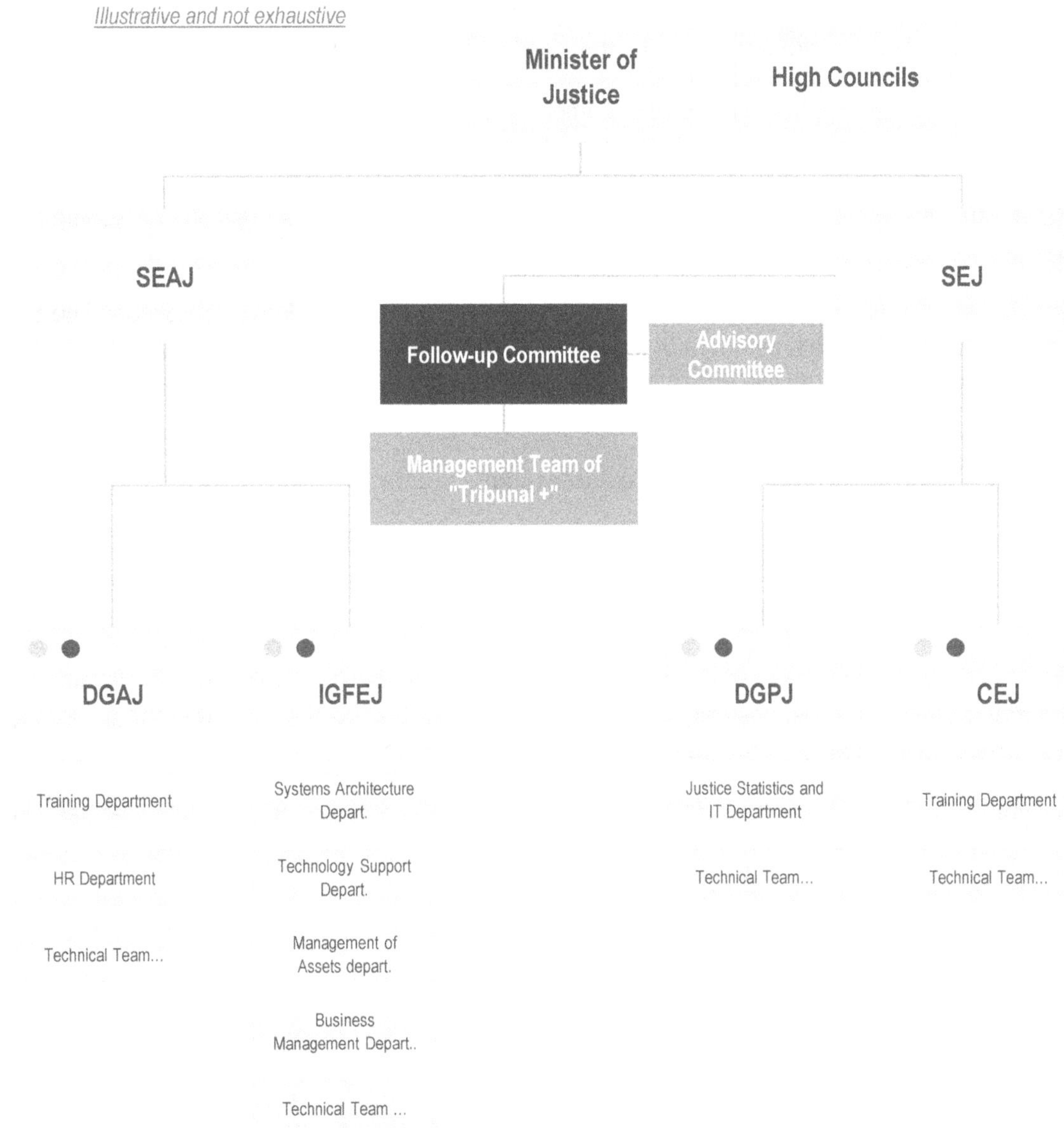

Source: Data provided by the Ministry of Justice of Portugal.

Notes

[1] Ratio between the number of disposed cases and the number of new cases during a given period.

[2] Ratio between number of pending cases and average number of resolved cases per day during the year, i.e. number of days needed for the court to resolve all pending cases at the current pace.

[3] See the impact of the introduction of the new Code of Civil Procedure on pendency rates.

[4] See the separation of enforcement cases that depend on actions from the court.

[5] Note by Turkey: The information in this document with reference to "Cyprus" relates to the southern part of the Island. There is no single authority representing both Turkish and Greek Cypriot people on the Island. Turkey recognises the Turkish Republic of Northern Cyprus (TRNC). Until a lasting and equitable solution is found within the context of the United Nations, Turkey shall preserve its position concerning the "Cyprus issue".

Note by all the European Union Member States of the OECD and the European Union: The Republic of Cyprus is recognised by all members of the United Nations with the exception of Turkey. The information in this document relates to the area under the effective control of the Government of the Republic of Cyprus.

[6] The results of the Sintra pilot project were assessed in Deloitte (2016)'s interim evaluation.

[7] Information provided by Ministry of Justice, DGPJ Statistics.

[8] The new Code of Civil Procedure introduces a distinction between enforcement cases that are pending on a decision or action by the court and cases pending on actions by other parties or on the expiry of a period. The change, which is yet to be implemented in case statistics, will allow to distinguish pendent cases that fall within the responsibility of the court from those that do not and make the pendency rates of Portuguese courts easier to compare to those of other countries.

[9] This impact assessment method is often called "difference in differences". For a further description, see Gertler (2011).

[10] Enforcement cases in civil and commercial courts of first instance.

References

CEPEJ (2018), "European judicial systems – Efficiency and quality of justice", CEPEJ Studies, No. 26. European Commission for the Efficiency of Justice, Council of Europe.

Deloitte (2016), "Tribunal+ Relatório intercalar de impacto", Tribunal + project document, preliminary version.

European Commission (2018), "Public opinion in the European Union", Standard Eurobarometer 82, Vol. A: Countries, http://data.europa.eu/euodp/en/data/dataset/S2215_90_3_STD90_ENG.

European Commission (2018), "Public opinion in the European Union", Standard Eurobarometer 90, Vol. A: Countries, http://data.europa.eu/euodp/en/data/dataset/S2215_90_3_STD90_ENG.

Gertler, P. (2011), *Impact Evaluation in Practice*, First Edition, The World Bank.

Ministry of Justice of Portugal (2018), "Monitoring the consolidation process on the implementation of the pilot-scheme Tribunal + and roll out preparation at national level'", Tribunal + project document.

OECD (2019), *OECD Economic Surveys: Portugal 2019,* OECD Publishing, Paris, https://doi.org/10.1787/eco_surveys-prt-2019-en.

OECD (2010), *Making Reform Happen: Lessons from OECD Countries*, OECD Publishing, Paris, https://doi.org/10.1787/9789264086296-en.

Portuguese Justice System (2019), *Medidas concluídas vs desenvolvimento do Plano Justiça mais Próxima*, https://partilha.justica.gov.pt/Transparencia/Dados-e-Estatisticas/-Medidas-concluidas-vs-execucao-do-Plano-Justica-mais-Proxima.

WHO (2010), *Nine Steps for Developing a Scaling-up Strategy*, World Health Organization, www.who.int/immunization/hpv/deliver/nine_steps_for_developing_a_scalingup_strategy_who_2010.pdf.

Annex A. The national court system in Portugal

The organisation of the court system

The constitution of Portugal establishes the organisation of the Portuguese courts and divides it into two different jurisdictions: the judicial courts and the administrative and fiscal courts. The constitution also makes provisions regarding the Constitutional Court, the Audit Court, the arbitration tribunals, the justice of the peace courts and conflict courts (Figure A.1):

- The *judicial courts* are common courts which deal with civil and criminal issues, with jurisdiction in all matters not allocated to other judicial bodies.
- The *administrative and tax courts* are competent to settle disputes arising out of administrative and tax legal relations.
- The *Audit Court* is the body with authority to scrutinise the legality of public expenditure.
- The *Constitutional Court* is the body entrusted specifically with the administration of justice in matters of a legal-constitutional nature.
- The *Conflict Court* settles jurisdictional conflicts between judicial and administrative courts.[1]
- The *arbitration centres* are mainly private entities.
- The *peace courts* are competent to decide on those actions with values that does not exceed EUR 15 000.

Figure A.1. The organisation of the judiciary in Portugal

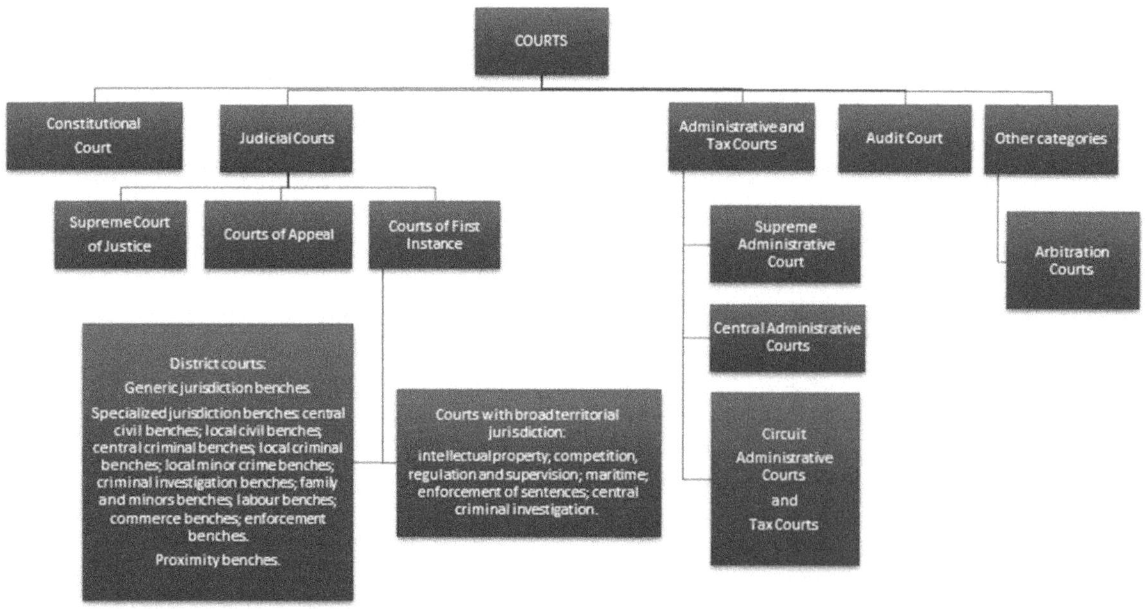

COURTS

Constitutional Court

Judicial Courts

Administrative and Tax Courts

Audit Court

Other categories

Supreme Court of Justice

Courts of Appeal

Courts of First Instance

Supreme Administrative Court

Central Administrative Courts

Circuit Administrative Courts and Tax Courts

Arbitration Courts

District courts:
Generic jurisdiction benches.
Specialized jurisdiction benches: central civil benches; local civil benches; central criminal benches; local criminal benches; local minor crime benches; criminal investigation benches; family and minors benches; labour benches; commerce benches; enforcement benches.
Proximity benches.

Courts with broad territorial jurisdiction:
intellectual property; competition, regulation and supervision; maritime; enforcement of sentences; central criminal investigation.

Source: Provided by the Ministry of Justice of Portugal, 2019

The national territory is divided into 23 judicial demarcations (*comarcas*), which correspond to the administrative districts. Each judicial demarcation comprises multiple municipalities. The central units of the demarcation courts have competency in the entire territory of the judicial county or for a larger group of municipalities. The local units, on the other hand, have competency for one or a small group of municipalities within the judicial demarcation.

Under Articles 209 *et seq.* of its constitution, Portugal has two separate sets of courts – the civil courts and the administrative courts. Provision is also made for other courts – the Constitutional Court (*Tribunal Constitucional*), the Court of Auditors (*Tribunal de Contas*), courts of arbitration (*tribunais arbitrais*) and justices of the peace (*julgados de paz*).

In the civil sphere, the ordinary courts with civil and criminal jurisdiction are the judicial courts, which are organised in three instances. In descending order of hierarchical rank and territorial scope, these are: the Supreme Court (*Supremo Tribunal de Justiça*, with jurisdiction over the whole country), the courts of appeal (*tribunais da relação*, one per judicial district and two in the Porto judicial district) and the district courts (*tribunais de comarca,* at first instance).

The judicial courts of first instance fall into three categories, depending on the subject matter of the action and the amount at stake: courts with general jurisdiction, specialised jurisdiction (criminal cases, family matters, minors, labour law, commercial, maritime courts, intellectual property, penitentiary and competition and regulation and the enforcement of cases) or specific jurisdiction (civil, criminal or mixed divisions; civil or criminal benches; civil or criminal benches dealing with minor matters).

The administrative courts include the first instance administrative and tax courts, the central administrative courts (North and South) and the Supreme Administrative Court (*Supremo Tribunal Administrativo*, covering the whole country).

Conflicts of jurisdiction between courts are resolved by a *Tribunal de Conflitos*, regulated by law.[2]

Court management

Courts of first instance

The management of each judicial court of first instance is carried out by a management board (*conselho de gestão*), presided over by a presiding judge. The board has a tripartite structure composed by the presiding judge, a co-ordinating prosecutor and the judicial administrator. In this management structure, each intervening party has its own powers. The presiding judge must communicate with the High Council of the Judiciary, the co-ordinating prosecutor with the High Council of the Public Prosecution, and the judiciary administrator with the Ministry of Justice (through the Directorate-General for the Administration of Justice). Certain matters are reserved for deliberation by the management board. As regards the judicial courts of first instance, the High Council for the Judiciary and the Prosecutor General, in co-operation with the Minister of Justice, establish, in their respective remits of competency, the strategic goals for the performance of the judicial courts of first instance over a three-year period and monitor compliance with those goals on a yearly basis. A similar mechanism applies to prosecutors.

The activity of each court is monitored throughout the judicial year, with quarterly meetings between representatives of the High Council of the Judiciary, the High Council of the Public Prosecution and the competent department of the Ministry of Justice, to follow up on the evolution of the results registered regarding the objectives that were established.

The Ministry of Justice authorises the opening of public competitions for access to the career of a judge, to be carried out by the Centre for Judicial Studies (induction and in-service continuous training institution for judges and prosecutors). The recruitment of court officials is managed by the Directorate-General for the Administration of Justice of the Ministry of Justice.

Appellate and Supreme Courts

Appellate courts and the Supreme Court are headed by a judge, elected by the seating judges of the respective courts and their administrative tasks are limited to supervising court services and guaranteeing its normal functioning, by delivering the necessary service orders. Besides those administrative tasks, presiding judges of the appellate courts and the Supreme Court also have jurisdictional attributions, such as to decide on competency conflicts between different units of the court.

At the administrative and fiscal jurisdiction, the management competencies of the presiding judges of the appellate and Supreme Courts are wider. For instance, the president of a Central Administrative Court or the president of the Administrative Supreme Court can: propose to the High Council for the Administrative and Fiscal Courts the criteria that should be applied in the distribution of cases among judges; plan and organise court human resources, aiming for an adequate distribution of workload per judge; reallocate cases whenever there is a modification of the number of judges; and temporarily reallocate judges when needed.

At the national level, the managing powers lie with the High Council of the Judiciary and the Prosecutor General, in co-operation with the Minister of Justice. As regards the administrative and tax courts of first instance, the management powers at the national level lie with the High Council for the Administrative and Tax Courts and, at the local level, with the presiding judge of each court of first instance and the judicial administrator (in courts with more than ten judges) or with the secretary of the court (in courts with less than ten judges).

The UN Human Rights Council's Special Rapporteur on the independence of judges and lawyers, in her 10 June 2015 report, concluded by calling on Portugal to: i) promote the greater managerial administrative autonomy of justice institutions; ii) ensure adequate capacity of the Superior Council of the Magistracy and the Public Prosecution; iii) increase investment in the promotion of access to justice; iv) ensure dedicated attention to victims of violence; and v) invest in the training of judges, prosecutors and lawyers.[3]

The UN Special Rapporteur cited above "believes that the management and maintenance of the electronic system of the database of the courts should be under the entire responsibility of the judicial bodies. This independence from the executive will enhance the independence of the entire judicial system and its accountability, in particular regarding the management of confidential information".

High judicial councils and human resources management of the judiciary

Recruitment, promotion and incompatibilities

Access to the profession of judge is a three-stage process comprising a public entrance examination, a theoretical and practical training course undertaken at the Centre for Judicial Studies (*Centro de Estudos Judiciários*), and an apprenticeship. If a candidate successfully completes all three stages, he/she will be appointed as a trial court judge at courts of first instance (*Juízes de Direito)*. Judges continue their training throughout their career.

There are two high judicial councils: the High Council of the Judiciary (*Conselho Superior da Magistratura*) conducts regular inspections at the courts of first instance, and the High Council for the Administrative and Tax Courts (*Conselho Superior dos Tribunais Administrativos e Fiscais*) does the same for judges at these courts. Following each inspection, judges are ranked by merit, using the categories "very good", "good with distinction", "good", "sufficient" and "mediocre". If a judge is ranked in the "mediocre" category, they will be suspended from duty and an inquiry will be launched to assess their suitability for the job.

The High Council of the Judiciary and the High Council for the Administrative and Tax Courts are responsible for appointing, assigning, transferring, promoting and taking disciplinary action in respect of judges of the judicial courts and the administrative and tax courts.

To ensure that judges are independent and impartial, the constitution stipulates that practising judges may not carry out any other duties, be they public or private, with the exception of unpaid teaching or scientific research in the field of law. Judges can only be transferred, suspended, retired or dismissed in the cases provided for by law; they may not be held accountable for their decisions in adjudicating cases, other than where the law provides for exceptions.

Performance appraisal and discipline

The performance appraisal criteria of judges are personal attributes and qualities, including those required for performing the judicial function (dignity, independence, ethics, acceptance and comprehension of the environment in which the judge is serving, maintenance of good professional relations, a sense of justice), intellectual and professional capacities (a high intellectual level, ability to comprehend concrete legal situations, good quality of work), organisational abilities and an ability to adapt to the function.

The performance appraisal of Portuguese judges is regulated by the Statute of Judicial Magistrates and the Regulation on the Judicial Inspection of the Judicial High Council of the Judiciary. Disciplinary proceedings are regulated in the same way. This inspection body (Judicial Assessment Service) is made of some 20 inspectors who are former judges from the courts of appeal, with more than 20 years of experience as judges. Each inspector has a secretary for administrative tasks, such as collecting the judicial proceedings or court statistics that the inspector will need to evaluate the productivity and efficiency rates of the judge who is under performance evaluation. This regular performance appraisal is carried out after each judge's first year in office and then every four years. Extraordinary appraisals can be carried out whenever the High Judicial Council deems necessary.

The marks awarded can be Mediocre, Sufficient, Good and Very Good. These are based on the following criteria: mode and volume of work, difficulty and management of the service for which he/she is in charge, his/her ability to simplify pleadings, professional development and training, intellectual profile, published legal works, civic aptitude and others. The appraisal leads to a detailed report with a mark proposal, which has to be ratified (or not) by the High Judicial Council, prior to a hearing of the incumbent. The decision of the High Judicial Council may be appealed before the Supreme Court. The Supreme Court has traditionally been reluctant to review the facts of the case in disciplinary proceedings by primarily relying on the conclusions the judicial inspection report. This may hamper judicial independence by biasing the factual narrative of the decision in favour of the judicial inspection. This issue was addressed also by the European Court of Human Rights in a recent ruling.[4] Moreover, the review regime for disciplinary procedures has been changed in the new Judicial Magistrates Bylaw, which is being discussed in parliament.

Notes

[1] Law of 1931 (Decree 19243 of 16 January 1931, amended by Decree 19438 of 11 March 1931 and Decree-Law 23185 of 30 October 1933).

[2] This discussion is based on a description of the judicial system of Portugal, European e-Justice Portal: https://e-justice.europa.eu/content_judicial_systems_in_member_states-16-pt-en.do?member=1.

[3] The Magistrates' Union of the Public Prosecutor's Office: www.smmp.pt/wp-content/uploads/Grabiela-Knaul-Visita-de-2015.pdf.

[4] Ramos Nunes de Carvalho e Sá v. Portugal, judgement of 6 November 2018 (Grand Chamber), http://hudoc.echr.coe.int/eng-press?i=003-6242630-8119316.

Reference

UN (2015), *Report of the Special Rapporteur on the independence of judges and lawyers, Gabriela Knaul, Addendum, Mission to Portugal*, United Nations Human Rights Council, A/HRC/29/26/Add.4, https://documents-dds-ny.un.org/doc/UNDOC/GEN/G15/136/97/PDF/G1513697.pdf?OpenElement.

www.ingramcontent.com/pod-product-compliance
Lightning Source LLC
LaVergne TN
LVHW081414110826
845149LV00010B/1742
* 9 7 8 9 2 6 4 4 6 1 9 7 0 *